THE
BRITISH AND AMERICAN
DRAMA OF TO-DAY

OUTLINES FOR THEIR STUDY

Suggestions, Questions, Biographies and Bibliographies
for use in connection with the study of
the more important plays

By
BARRETT H. CLARK

Author of "European Theories of the Drama,"
"Contemporary French Dramatists,"
"Four Plays of the Free Theater," etc.

AMS PRESS
NEW YORK

Reprinted from the edition of 1921, Cincinnati

First AMS EDITION published 1971

Manufactured in the United States of America

International Standard Book Number: 0-404-01547-6

Library of Congress Catalog Number: 76-155635

AMS PRESS INC.
NEW YORK, N.Y.   10003

To
BRANDER MATTHEWS
This Book Is
Gratefully Dedicated

PREFACE TO NEW EDITION OF
BRITISH AND AMERICAN DRAMA OF TODAY

THIS book was written for one purpose, and one alone. A friend of mine surprised me by reading it from page three to the end, and remarked that he thought it rather poor: it was not complete, he claimed, it contained questions that remained unanswered, and finally, it was decidedly obvious. My friend was a critic and his knowledge of the modern theater was fairly extensive.

My author's pride was hurt and I stiffly asked him whether he had read the preface. He had not. Had he read the Preface to "The Continental Drama of Today," the earlier companion volume? He had not read that, either. I referred him to the opening lines: "A growing demand on the part of clubs, reading circles, schools, colleges and universities for definite and systematic guidance in the study of the modern movement in drama has led me to compile this Outline," etc. The second volume was merely an extension of the first, based upon the same premises and written for the same purpose.

My friend read the preface and admitted that he was in the wrong. These books are not for specialists, and they are not for dramatists. They are simply aids, and it is hoped, stimulants for lay students of the theater and the printed play.

It was my purpose to provide outlines for the study of a number of more or less representative modern dramatists. I have asked questions in order to stimulate thought and discussion. I have often been requested to answer these questions. Many of them I cannot answer; if I could, I should have written another book, for a correct answer would solve certain problems that most critics ought to be, but are far from, clear about.

The demand for these books appears to persist, otherwise there would be no necessity for this new preface. But I welcome the chance to add a word to my critical utterances of over five years ago:

There is much in this book that I would change if it were not that any attempt at modification would destroy the unity and (with such value as it has) the scheme of study for the pursuit of which the book was first designed. However, I must ask the reader to remember that he must not take too seriously my dogmatic assertions. Perhaps I ought not to admit it, but today I am not quite so sure about many of the dramatic canons I so freely enunciated a few years ago as a good pedagogue ought to be. I trust I have safely passed through the period of pedagoguery, though I am still irritated by receiving letters addressed to me as "Professor." I will admit that I believe dramatic technique to be neither so mechanical a matter as I claimed it was, nor the Rules of the Drama so rigid as I would have my readers think—five years ago. And finally (with my publisher's permission) I greatly fear that I am neither so infallible nor so eminent an authority on the drama as I (thought I) was when I wrote the book.

February 1, 1921   B. H. C.

PREFACE

" The British and American Drama of To-day "
aims to complete the series of suggestive study
outlines of representative modern plays begun in
" The Continental Drama of To-day." The same
general form and method have been followed as
were employed in the first volume, with the exception of two or three slight modifications.
First, owing either to the persistent refusal of
certain dramatists to publish their plays, because
of practical considerations or because they have
no wish to make known their works through the
medium of the printed page, dramatists like Eugene Walter, David Belasco, and George M.
Cohan are but briefly referred to. In rarer instances, that of Sir James Barrie for example, the
best and most typical plays are either not printed
or, if such was the case, in *éditions de luxe*, the
price of which is prohibitive.

The selection of plays has been a rather difficult task. It has, of course, been impossible to
consider all plays of importance or to include the
best of each dramatist. Some authors have not
even been touched upon. Israel Zangwill, Rudolf
Besier, Charles Rann Kennedy, Alfred Sutro, and

Somerset Maugham are not truly representative: the first three are rather exceptional than typical, the last two are typical, but their work is already represented by that of such men as Pinero, Jones, and Davies. It has been my aim only to include typical plays of typical dramatists, thereby affording the student a general view of the dramatic movement in English-speaking countries since its inception something over a quarter of a century ago.

The recent dramatic movement in Ireland has very little to do with that in England, but my inclusion of outlines on Irish plays under the general title of " British " may be excused as a matter of expediency and geography, " British " being understood to embrace the British Isles.

The mention of first American performances of English plays is, I hope, an aid, but I am fully aware of the deficiency in this branch of my work. There are no complete and authentic records containing the necessary information.

It would be impossible to express here my thanks to all those who have helped me in the compilation of this volume. I may, however, mention that among the authors who have tendered personal aid are: Mr. Bernard Shaw, Mr. William Butler Yeats, Lady Gregory, Mr. St. John G. Ervine, Mr. Henry Arthur Jones, Mr. George Moore, Mr. Granville Barker, Mr. John Galsworthy, and Mr. George Middleton. To Mr. T. C. Murray, Mr. Hubert Henry Davies, Miss Githa Sowerby, Miss Elizabeth Baker, Mr. Stephen Phillips, and Mr. J. O. Francis, I am indebted for courteous co-operation by letter. Mr. William Archer, Mr. J. T. Grein, and Mr. Clayton Hamilton have also given valuable advice. Mr. Montrose J. Moses and Mr. T. R. Edwards have been unsparing in their efforts to make the bibliographies as complete and free from error as possible.

B. H. C.

CONTENTS

THE ENGLISH DRAMA

THE IRISH DRAMA

THE AMERICAN DRAMA

CONTENTS

THE ENGLISH DRAMA

ARTHUR PINERO

Arthur Wing Pinero—since 1909, Sir Arthur Pinero—was born in London in 1855. Like many another dramatist, he was forced to study law. Pinero's father, himself a lawyer, put his young son into his office, where the youth, much against his will, remained until the age of nineteen. In 1874, he was engaged by Mr. and Mrs. Wyndham, and acted small parts for a year in Edinburgh. After a year's acting the theater burned down, but he secured employment in Liverpool, and in 1876 came to London, acting at the Globe Theater. Not long after, he entered Irving's company and remained at the Lyceum for five years. During this time the young actor, not a very good one from all accounts, was writing plays, and in 1877 his first, " £200 a Year," was produced at the Globe. " Daisy's Escape" and " Bygones " were soon after performed at the Lyceum. It was probably the success of " Daisy's Escape," together with the assurance that he would never make a great actor, which led Pinero to abandon the stage. His earlier efforts are practically negligible; they are imitative, stiff, and conventional. " The Money-Spinner " is sometimes regarded as indicative of the dramatist's later skill, but not until the production of " The Squire " (1881) did some promise of better things emerge. The following year, William Archer spoke of the author as "a thoughtful and conscientious writer with artistic aims, if not yet with full command of his artistic means." With "The Magistrate," "The Schoolmistress," and "Dandy Dick" —all farces—Pinero attracted considerable attention, while "Sweet Lavender" (1888), with its sentiment and tears, brought him fame. Beginning with "The Profligate" (1889), Pinero opened a period of great fecundity: farces, dramas, and comedies succeeded one another for many years, and established standards which were to obtain for over a decade. "The Second Mrs. Tanqueray" (1893) was rightly considered the finest English play of the time. Of late, Sir Arthur has turned to the depiction of sections of middle-class life (in "The Thunderbolt" especially); this play, together with "Mid-Channel" (1909), has met with little success, though the later manner of the dramatist is undoubtedly more mature, more skilful and artistic than that even of "Mrs. Tanqueray" and "Iris." Still more recently have come genre pictures like "The 'Mind-the-Paint' Girl" and "Preserving Mr. Panmure," but on the whole these are less satisfactory than such works as "The Gay Lord Quex."

Pinero is a technician par excellence. His mastery of plot-construction, his ability to create and maintain suspense, are indisputably admirable. His creation of character, especially in "The Benefit of the Doubt," "Lady Bountiful," "The Gay Lord Quex," and "The Thunderbolt," is masterly and convincing. Yet on the whole Pinero's plays, by reason of their occasional falsity to life, their too conventional structure, their dialogue, which is in places exceedingly stilted, fall short of true greatness.

PLAYS

£200 A YEAR (1877).

THE COMET (1878).

DAISY'S ESCAPE (1879).

HESTER'S MYSTERY (1880).

BYGONES (1880).

THE MONEY-SPINNER (1880).

Performed at Wallack's Theater, New York 1882.

IMPRUDENCE (1881).

Performed at the Boston Museum 1882.

THE SQUIRE (1881).

Performed at Daly's Theater, New York 1882.

GIRLS AND BOYS (1882).

Performed at Daly's Theater, New York 1883.

THE RECTOR (1883).

Performed at the Boston Museum 1883.

LORDS AND COMMONS (1883).

Performed at Daly's Theater, New York 1885.

THE ROCKET (1883).

LOW WATER (1884).

IN CHANCERY (1884).

Performed at the Madison Square Theater, New York 1885.

THE MAGISTRATE (1885).

Performed at Daly's Theater, New York 1885.

THE SCHOOLMISTRESS (1886).

Performed at the Standard Theater, New York 1887.

THE HOBBY-HORSE (1886).

    Performed at the Knickerbocker Theater, New York 1887.

DANDY DICK (1887).

    Performed at Daly's Theater, New York 1887.

SWEET LAVENDER (1888).

    Performed at Daly's Theater, New York 1888.

THE WEAKER SEX (1888).

    Performed by the Kendals on their American tour, 1890.

THE PROFLIGATE (1889).

    Performed at Wallack's Theater, New York 1900.

THE CABINET MINISTER (1890).

    Performed at Daly's Theater, New York 1892.

LADY BOUNTIFUL (1891).

    Performed at the Lyceum Theater, New York 1891 and at the Boston Museum.

THE TIMES (1891).

THE AMAZONS (1893).

    Performed at the Lyceum Theater, New York 1894.

THE SECOND MRS. TANQUERAY (1893).

    Performed by the Kendals, Star Theater, New York 1893, and later by Mrs. Patrick Campbell.

THE NOTORIOUS MRS. EBBSMITH (1895).

    Performed by Sir John Hare, Abbey's Theater, New York 1895.

THE BENEFIT OF THE DOUBT (1895).

    Performed at the Lyceum Theater, New York 1896.

THE PRINCESS AND THE BUTTERFLY (1897).

    Performed at the Lyceum Theater, New York 1897.

TRELAWNEY OF THE 'WELLS' (1898).

Performed at the Lyceum Theater, New York 1898.

THE GAY LORD QUEX (1899).

Performed by Sir John Hare at the Criterion Theater, New York 1900.

IRIS (1901).

Performed at the Criterion Theater, New York 1902.

LETTY (1903).

Performed at the Hudson Theater, New York 1904.

A WIFE WITHOUT A SMILE (1904).

Performed at the Empire Theater, New York 1904.

HIS HOUSE IN ORDER (1906).

Performed at the Empire Theater, New York, 1906.

THE THUNDERBOLT (1908).

Performed at the New Theater, New York 1910, and by the Drama Players on tour 1912-3.

MID-CHANNEL (1909).

Performed, with Ethel Barrymore, at the Empire Theater, New York 1910.

PRESERVING MR. PANMURE (1911).

Performed, with Gertrude Elliott, New York, and on tour 1911-2.

THE "MIND-THE-PAINT" GIRL (1912).

Performed, with Billie Burke, at the Lyceum Theater, New York, and on tour 1912-3.

THE WIDOW OF WASDALE HEAD (1912).

PLAYGOERS (1913).

(Three or four adaptations and a libretto are not included in the above list.)

Walter H. Baker of Boston publishes the following: "The Magistrate," "The Schoolmistress," "The Hobby-Horse," "Sweet Lavender," "The Weaker Sex," "The Profligate," "The Cabinet Minister," "Lady Bountiful," "The Times," "The Amazons," "The Second Mrs. Tanqueray," "The Notorious Mrs. Ebbsmith," "The Gay Lord Quex," "Iris," "Letty," "A Wife Without a Smile," "His House in Order," "The Thunderbolt," "Mid-Channel," and "Preserving Mr. Panmure." The Dramatic Publishing Company (Sergel) publishes: "The Benefit of the Doubt" and "Trelawney of the 'Wells.'" Samuel French publishes: "The Money-Spinner," "The Squire," "The Rocket," "In Chancery," "Hester's Mystery," and "The Princess and the Butterfly." The rest of the early plays are unobtainable. "The 'Mind-the-Paint' Girl" is published by William Heinemann, London; "Playgoers" by Samuel French. "The Widow of Wasdale Head" is not yet published. "The Second Mrs. Tanqueray" is included in "Chief Contemporary Dramatists" (Houghton Mifflin).

REFERENCES: Hamilton Fyfe, "Arthur Wing Pinero" (Greening & Co., London); William Archer, "Real Conversations" (Heinemann, London), "About the Theater" (Unwin, London), "English Dramatists of To-day" (Sampson Low, London), "The Theatrical World" (Walter Scott, London), "Playmaking" (Small, Maynard); Mario Borsa,

" The English Stage of To-day " (Lane); Augustin
Filon, " The English Stage " (Dodd, Mead); Oscar
Heermann, " Living Dramatists " (Brentano); E. E.
Hale, Jr., " Dramatists of To-day " (Holt); George
Moore, " Impressions and Opinions " (Brentano);
Ashley Dukes, " Modern Dramatists " (Dramatic
Publishing Co.); P. P. Howe, " Dramatic Portraits "
(Kennerley); Bernard Shaw, " Dramatic Opinions
and Essays " (Brentano); A. B. Walkley, " Drama
and Life " (Brentano), " Playhouse Impressions "
(Unwin, London); Frank Wadleigh Chandler, " As-
pects of Modern Drama " (Macmillan); H. M. Wal-
brook, " Nights at the Play " (Ham-Smith, London);
Cecil F. Armstrong, " From Shakespere to Shaw "
(Mills and Boon, London); Clayton Hamilton,
" Studies in Stagecraft " (Holt), " The Theory of
the Theater " (Holt); Brander Matthews, " Inquiries
and Opinions " (Scribner), " A Study of the Drama "
(Houghton Mifflin); Arthur Pinero, " Robert Louis
Stevenson, the Dramatist " (Columbia University);
Ludwig   Lewisohn,   " The   Modern   Drama "
(Huebsch).—*Magazines: Munsey,* vol. x (p. 247);
Book-buyer, vol. xvii (p. 301); *Forum,* vol. xxvi (p.
119), vol. xlvii (p. 494); *Blackwood's,* vol. clxvii (p.
837); *The Theatre,* vol. xxxiv (p. 3); *Nation,* vol.
lxxxiii (p. 211); *North American Review,* vol.
clxxxviii (p. 38); *Critic,* vol. xxxvii (p. 117); *The-
atre,* vol. xxxvii (p. 346); *Collier's,* vol. xlviii (p. 34);
Living Age, vol. cclxxviii (p. 265).

SWEET LAVENDER

A domestic drama in three acts. First performed
in 1888.

" Sweet Lavender " is one of the most popular of
Pinero's plays. In London it achieved the phenom-
enal record, for those days, of a run of 683 nights,
and on its revival not long after, of 737 nights. Since
that time it has been seen in America, Canada, Russia,
South Africa, Australia, Germany, and Italy. Its
success is attributable to its genial, if mawkish, sentiment, its optimism, and its kindly humor. In the
light of the dramatist's later works, it appears old-
fashioned and conventional in the extreme.

1. Probably no fitter play could be named to
typify the comedy of sentiment than " Sweet
Lavender." Pinero calls it a " domestic drama."
It is not that, at least in the sense that Giacosa's
" As the Leaves " or Ibsen's " John Gabriel Bork-
man " are domestic dramas. Pinero's play touches
merely the externals of life, deftly it is true, and
with an occasional semblance of reality, but the
dramatist's sympathy led him far astray both
from human nature and from the truth that lies
at the bottom of all things. This play should be

10

studied first for its occasional touches of characterization, then for the skill with which the author has constructed his story.

2. Pinero's chief contribution to the theater of his time will be doubtless found to consist of a series of plays in which the stories are, as a whole, well thought out, interesting, ingenious, and economical in the technical sense of the term. He will be considered a consummate craftsman, but his comments on life and human character must take second place. He is not, however, negligible in this capacity: there are far too convincing proofs to the contrary. In the present play Dick Phenyl is a case in question. The part is an especially rich one for a good actor, and can be made even more sympathetic on the stage than it is in print. Although he shares with the other characters in the play the annoying mannerism of speaking much too often in figurative language, he is still an affable fellow. Bulger, too, and Mrs. Gilfillian, are good minor sketches. The latter is a faint approximation to the Lady Bracknell and Duchess of Berwick types of Oscar Wilde. Her speech (p. 48) in the first act is distinctly Wildesque: "Innocent-looking! Do you think I will have my plans—my plans and my brother's —frustrated by a girl with ulterior motives and eyes like saucers?"

3. The various works * on the technic of the drama practically agree on the division of a play into five parts: exposition, development, climax, *dénouement*, and catastrophe. Aristotle more succinctly said that a play must have a beginning, a middle, and an end. Most plays can be satisfactorily so analyzed. " Sweet Lavender " presents an interesting clinical subject in its *dénouement*. Trace, in the third act, the numerous threads introduced in the first and second: Wedderburn's relations with Mrs. Rolt, Minnie's with Bream, Clement's with Lavender. Notice how the supposed failure of Wedderburn is smoothed over, how the coincidences are made to appear a little less improbable than they would be without the dramatic preparation. Mr. Delaney's " Come, I'll tell ye how I put the pieces of the puzzle together " is a good text for this analysis.

4. The end is " happy," that is, lovers are united, obstacles overcome, even at the expense of verisimilitude and the canons of ordinary morality. Undoubtedly the English public of the day

* Freytag, " The Technique of the Drama "; Elizabeth Woodbridge, " The Drama, Its Law and Technique "; W. T. Price, " The Analysis of Play Construction and Dramatic Principle," and " The Technique of the Drama "; Brander Matthews, " A Study of the Drama "; Clayton Hamilton, " The Theory of the Theater "; William Archer, " Playmaking "; Barrett H. Clark, " The Continental Drama of To-day "; George P. Baker, " The Technique of the Drama " (Houghton Mifflin).

demanded this and few dramatists dared face the
logical outcome of a situation of the sort. Five
years later, however, Pinero did carry out an
unpleasant theme, fearlessly: the success of " The
Second Mrs. Tanqueray " is but another proof of
the steady intellectual advance of the British theater public. But a curious instance of the dramatist's wavering between personal conviction and
his fear of the public is to be found in " The
Profligate " (1889). Read this play, comparing
the two endings: that of the acted version, which
ends in reconciliation, and the original, terminat-
ing in suicide.

THE SECOND MRS. TANQUERAY

A play in four acts. First performed in 1893.

" The Second Mrs. Tanqueray " marked a decided
step in advance of the drama of its day. To realize
just how far in advance one must read some of its
predecessors. One critic spoke of it as epoch-making,
and William Archer, always reserved and careful in
his judgments, disagreed with him only so far as to
state that no single play could make that pretension,
but that this one was a work " which Dumas might
sign without a blush." The admirable construction,
deep insight, and philosophical import of the theme,
if not the characters, make of " The Second Mrs.
Tanqueray " one of the finest dramatic achievements
of the past two decades.

1. The exposition has often been admired.
Each step is prepared with the utmost skill, and
the story of Aubrey's venture is unfolded before
our eyes in a manner that is interesting and
amusing. The first point to notice is that there
is none of the obvious mannered conversation which
is to be found in " Sweet Lavender." Pinero has
left behind him those threadbare devices which
introduced the history of his characters in a few
lines: ". . . I, Edmund Bulger, widower, have

loved you, Mrs. Ruth Rolt, widow, ever since
you fust set foot in the Temple, fifteen years
ago, a-bearing your two-year-old baby in your
arms, ma'am." But, in "The Second Mrs. Tanqueray," by means of an apparently casual conversation, taking place at a natural meeting of
Aubrey's friends, his past, his intentions, the re-
lationship among the men and their wives,—all
is made unmistakably clear.

If this exposition is in many ways admirable,
and if "The Second Mrs. Tanqueray " was an important milestone technically, it is necessary to
compare but one play of the past five years—Galsworthy's " Justice "—to realize the advance made
since 1893. Or, turning to Pinero's own later
work: " The Thunderbolt," or " Mid-Channel."
In " The Thunderbolt," the exposition is the more
remarkable in that it not only seems *casual*, but
inevitable. " Mid-Channel," on the other hand, is
conventional in its opening, but the exposition is
briefer and more to the point than in the play now
under discussion.

Compare the expositions in these three plays
with that of " The Second Mrs. Tanqueray."
Galsworthy's play has scarcely any, but is one required? Could that of " The Second Mrs. Tanqueray " be summarily disposed of as is that of
" Mid-Channel "?

2. Pinero has always kept well abreast of the

times in theatrical wares. A severe but usually just critic * said of him: " No other hand . . . could supply so efficiently the actual demand. When in the fullness of time and honors, Sir Arthur Pinero has need of an epitaph, it may well be this: He kept the theaters open." Certain it is that his early plays were influenced by Robertson and Gilbert, that " The Second Mrs. Tanqueray " and the half-dozen plays of its sort that followed, were more or less influenced by Ibsen, and the critic above quoted adds that " perhaps it would not have been possible . . . to have achieved the first act of ' The Thunderbolt ' if the third act of ' The Voysey Inheritance ' had not shown him the way." Nevertheless Pinero, like Augustus Thomas, has been quick to detect the trend of public thought and feeling, and no less alert to take advantage of it and write a " play of the hour."

This timeliness is perhaps one of the most important elements of successful plays. In 1893, Ibsen was a new name in England; his plays were beginning to be translated, discussed, produced. The Independent Theater, under J. T. Grein, had produced " Ghosts " in 1891, and invoked a storm of invective from the press; Bernard Shaw was hurling thunderbolts at the British public in the columns of the *Saturday Review;* Henry Arthur

* P. P. Howe in " Dramatic Portraits " (Kennerley).

Jones was lecturing on the "Renascence of the Drama." It was the day of the New Woman. And Pinero wrote a powerful play around a woman with a past; five years previously, it is safe to say that the play would not have been successful. As it was, the time was ripe.

There is nothing reprehensible in the practice: the theater must attempt to treat of people, customs, and ideas of the day. In America it is undeniable that timeliness is carried to an extreme. After some sensational trial we may expect a welter of plays dealing with the subject, just as after the production of Brieux's "Damaged Goods," a number of plays, concerned more or less directly with the same theme, made their appearance. Let a play like "The Yellow Jacket" or "Alias Jimmy Valentine" enjoy a long run, and it is but a question of a few months before the market is likely to be glutted with Chinese and crook plays.

3. In his lecture on "R. L. Stevenson: the Dramatist," Pinero said: "What is dramatic talent? Is it not the power to project characters, and to cause them to tell an interesting story through the medium of dialogue? This is *dramatic* talent; and dramatic talent, if I may so express it, is the raw material of *theatrical* talent. Dramatic, like poetic, talent is born, not made; if it is to achieve success on the stage, it must be developed into

theatrical talent by hard study, and generally by long practice. For theatrical talent consists in the power of making your characters not only tell a story by means of dialogue, but to tell it in such skilfully devised form and order as shall, within the limits of an ordinary theatrical representation, give rise to the greatest possible amount of that peculiar kind of emotional effect the production of which is the one great function of the theater." Pinero is precisely the dramatist who has developed his dramatic into a thoroughly theatrical talent, by " hard study " and by " long practice." The transition may be best observed by comparing the " dramatic " " Sweet Lavender " with the " theatrical " " Second Mrs. Tanqueray."

IRIS

A drama in five acts. First performed in 1901.

In " The Second Mrs. Tanqueray " Pinero is content with placing before his audience a situation, and selecting a certain group of personages to work it out. In " Iris," although there is a situation, we are inclined to believe that the author wished to draw the picture of a woman, struggling with a situation, rather than a situation in which people struggle to extricate themselves. The earlier play was more of a story, the later, a painting. No such painting, it is true, as " Hedda Gabler," still it is as near to it as this dramatist ever came. " Iris " is justly acclaimed as one of the best technical feats of Pinero, for the story is simply and interestingly told, the character of the heroine carefully limned, the logical needs of the theme rigidly supplied.

1. In the case of " Iris," the exposition is of especial importance. Every step she takes in her downward course throughout the play is dependent upon (1) the conditions of the will, and (2) her character. These two points must be indelibly impressed upon the mind of the audience, or what follows will be unconvincing. Take careful note of the innumerable references to Iris's tempera-

ment; the opening scene, between Miss Pinsent and
Kane, is full of them, and when Iris herself enters
(p. 8) she adds to our store of knowledge. Kane's
". . . it is only fair to assume that your husband, *knowing how greatly your happiness depends upon personal comfort,* was actuated by a
desire to safeguard you" (the italics are mine) is
peculiarly significant. Iris even goes so far as to
quote some of the terms of the will.

Does Pinero succeed in convincing you of the
probability of the conditions? Does he prepare a
sufficiently solid foundation upon which to build
the rest of the structure? Is the exposition of
"Iris" more economical or less so than that of
"The Second Mrs. Tanqueray"? In what way is
it superior to that of "Sweet Lavender"? Compare it with the exposition of "Mid-Channel."

2. Pinero has selected a character more subtle
and more difficult to portray than Mrs. Tanqueray: Iris, a weak woman, taxes the dramatist's
powers far more than Paula, whose very strength
forms, as it were, a point of resistance against
which to build situations. Positive wills, active
agents, are the stuff of which drama is made, while
passive and negative ones present numerous obstacles for the maker of plays. In "The Second
Mrs. Tanqueray" the conflict of wills furnishes
ready-made material, in "Iris" the lack of will,
the drifting of the heroine, forces the dramatist

at every turn to invent situations; it calls upon him to exert all his ingenuity to keep the story moving.

Compare the two plays from this standpoint. Notice how carefully Pinero has built up his situations, and how each one reveals some side of the character of Iris.

3. The curtain falls nine times during this play. Nowadays it is the usual custom not to divide an act into scenes. What were Pinero's reasons? Does this division in any way detract from the dramatic effectiveness or the unity of the play? Is it a confession of weakness? Could the dramatist have managed as well without this frequent division? Does the process add to the interest and suspense?

4. Pinero is a master of dramaturgic devices. One example will here suffice: shortly after the opening of the fourth act occurs the following stage-direction:

(After some hesitation, he produces a bunch of keys and removes from it a latch-key. Weighing the key in his hand meditatively, he walks towards the settee; then he turns and tosses the key upon the table. . . . She picks up the key and, rising, drops it into a vase which stands upon the mantelpiece. The key strikes the bottom of the vase with a sharp sound. Having done this, she resumes her seat and sips her tea.)

The significance of the act is doubly impressed upon the audience; first Maldonado's detaching the key and throwing it upon the table, and second Iris's dropping it, " with a sharp sound," into the vase. This is a stroke of dramaturgic genius: it advances the plot and reveals character in a most masterly fashion. Find other instances of this in " Iris."

5. In the last act Pinero has the courage which he lacked in " Sweet Lavender," and which some critics declare he lacked when he made Paula Tanqueray commit suicide in order to escape: the courage to show the logical consequences of his story. Trenwith's return is bitter, as it should be, Iris's confession is wrung from the depths of her being. There is at least an element of true tragedy in Iris's final effort to retain Trenwith, and in her query, " Would the home have been ready for me? " and his answer, " Yes." Then comes Maldonado's denunciation of his mistress; she must leave. This, too, savors of tragedy, but after she leaves, and " *Maldonado utters a fierce cry and, with one movement of his arm, sweeps the china and bric-à-brac from the mantelpiece . . . overturns the table with a savage kick; then, raising a chair high in the air, he dashes it to the floor and breaks it into splinters . . .*"—is this in keeping with the spirit of the last scene? Of the whole play?

6. Eugene Walter's " The Easiest Way " * is in many respects similar to " Iris."   Compare the two plays.

* " The Easiest Way " has been printed only in a private edition, but it is often produced by stock companies.

MID-CHANNEL

A play in four acts. First performed in 1909.

As an example of the highest technical skill, of sound characterization, of a story well and interestingly unfolded, " Mid-Channel " must assume a position in the front rank of this dramatist's many works. It is one of the truest specimens of domestic drama produced in England.

1. Pinero once said * that after toiling at the superb exposition of " The Thunderbolt," he was determined not to go to the trouble of avoiding every possible incongruity and short-cut usually employed in conventional expositions, so that when he came to the opening of " Mid-Channel " he decided to convey the necessary information to his audience in a straightforward and more or less conventional manner. It was scarcely worth his while to conceal what must be obvious to nearly all his auditors: the effort to lay before them as quickly as possible that part of the character and past history of his personages which must be known before the play proper can begin. Conse-

* To Mr. Clayton Hamilton, who has courteously given me permission to print the above.

quently, almost the same ground is covered in a dozen pages which it took over sixty to cover in the preceding play.

If the exposition of " Mid-Channel " is rather conventional, compact, obvious, would the play have gained by the insertion of a long and possibly more skilful exposition? In other words, what is gained by the method here adopted? And what is lost?

2. The question, What is a tragedy? is considered in " The Continental Drama of To-day " (p. 152). Paul Hervieu says: " It is a play every part of which aims to create suspense, deep thinking, and pity. It is accompanied no longer, as of old, with magnificent draperies; it is a thing of the day, logical, prosaic, no longer bloody . . . the ways of fate are no longer manifested, as with the Greeks, in dreams, visions, or presentiments. Nowadays we try to show how the struggle for existence bears down inexorably upon those who are imprudent, too weak to defend themselves, those whose passions are stronger than their will power." This of course is peculiarly applicable to the plays of M. Hervieu himself, who has written tragedies according to his own formula. The French dramatist, as a rule, makes plays out of the human passions; with him the passions are usually sufficient in themselves to explain failure and tragedy. With the Anglo-Saxon this is not enough: if pas-

sions do work havoc with human lives, he is unwilling to offer that as the sole reason for failure; he must add external circumstances. Pinero in "Iris," however, accounts for the woman's ruin by her passion and her weakness, chiefly the latter, but he is careful to furnish a convenient Maldonado, who is an external force. The French dramatist can make his character declare, "C'est plus fort que moi!" and proceed with the happy assurance that he has sufficient motivation. Pinero is not an emotional dramatist, in the sense that Donnay and D'Annunzio are emotional; he must account for failure in some other way. In "Mid-Channel," Zoe gives us the reason for her failure and her husband's. She says: "It was doomed from the moment we agreed that we'd never be encumbered in our career with any—brats of children."

Nearly all Pinero's "dramas" are tearless: they are dramatic, effective, terrible at times, and possibly horrible, but only in the rarest instances, lachrymose. Perhaps this is the result of his English environment, and perhaps out of the fear that the British public dislikes any display of the deeper emotions, but Pinero prefers to be intellectual, in contradistinction to emotional, and wishes his plays to rest upon logic rather than upon passion. But it must be remembered that his characters are nearly all English.

3. The "Raisonneur" is a stock figure in many

of the plays of the nineteenth century, and in the plays of Dumas fils assumes an importance at times greatly out of keeping with the piece. In England, especially in the plays of Pinero and Henry Arthur Jones, he reappears as the middle-aged, kindly man-of-the-world, the adviser who invariably sets matters straight and administers stiff doses of good advice to the characters of the play, as well as to the audience. He is at once a dramatic expedient, a foil, and a relief-figure. In the hands of the actor for whom the part is written, he becomes a congenial link, as it were, between the audience and the characters. Some of the more striking instances are to be found in " The Liars," " Mrs. Dane's Defence," " The Case of Rebellious Susan," and " Dolly Reforming Herself," of Jones. In " Mid-Channel " it is Peter Mottram. Here, besides bringing about the temporary reconciliation between man and wife, he gives out the theme of the play (pp. 50-1), and offers a welcome relief to the sordidness of the rest of the piece.

Is there a character corresponding to Peter in " The Second Mrs. Tanqueray "? In " Sweet Lavender "?

4. The suicide in " Mid-Channel " is as inevitable as that of " Hedda Gabler " or " Justice." The dramatist has left no possible escape for the unfortunate woman. Trace the steps leading up

to the catastrophe. Is there a point in the play where matters could have been satisfactorily arranged? Could a logical change of heart have taken place in Theodore? Zoe being as she was, and Theodore remaining obdurate—in strict accordance with the character as we know him—could a reconciliation be made plausible?

HENRY ARTHUR JONES

Henry Arthur Jones was born at Grandborough, Bucks, in 1851. His early life was spent, and his primary education received in his native district. He went into business at Bradford and for some years was a commercial traveler. In 1878, at Exeter, he produced his first play, " Only 'Round the Corner." During the next few years he wrote a number of unimportant little plays, of which " A Clerical Error " (1879) was produced in London. In 1882, he wrote, in collaboration with Henry Herman, his first great success, the famous melodrama, " The Silver King," which has held the stage for thirty-three years, and shows no signs of aging. " Saints and Sinners " (1884) called forth the unstinted praise of Matthew Arnold. From that day to this Jones has, through his essays, lectures, and many plays, carried on a work which is of incalculable benefit for the English stage.

To Henry Arthur Jones, more than to any other single force, is due that Renascence and " uplift " —let the term be accepted in its best sense—of the contemporary English drama. Jones carries on the tradition of Congreve and Sheridan in high comedy. His best work, with the exception of " Michael and His Lost Angel," consists of comedies of manners. " The Liars," " The Case of Rebellious Susan," and " Dolly Reforming Herself," satires on contemporary society, are among the finest character plays of the day. Jones's work is characterized by close observation of the foibles of the upper classes and the aristocracy of England; a keen sense of humor—as opposed to the cleverness and wit of Wilde and Pinero —which brings him much closer to the English Restoration dramatists than any other of his day; and a keen sense of dramatic construction. Jones has written many comedies, but his melodramas—especially " The Silver King " and " The Middleman "—and his tragic play, " Michael and His Lost Angel "—must be taken into account in any estimate of the dramatist's total output.

PLAYS

ONLY 'ROUND THE CORNER (1878).

HEARTS OF OAK (1879).

HARMONY (1879).

ELOPEMENT (1879).

A CLERICAL ERROR (1879).

Performed at the Star Theater, New York 1886.

AN OLD MASTER (1881).

HIS WIFE (1881).

HOME AGAIN (1881).

A BED OF ROSES (1881).

THE SILVER KING (in collaboration with Henry Herman, 1882).

Performed at Wallack's Theater, New York 1883.

CHATTERTON (with Henry Herman, 1884).

Performed, with Wilson Barrett, at the Grand Opera House, New York 1886.

SAINTS AND SINNERS (1884).

Performed at the Madison Square Theater, New York 1885.

HOODMAN BLIND (in collaboration with Wilson Barrett, 1885).

Performed at Wallack's Theater, New York 1885.

THE LORD HARRY (with Wilson Barrett, 1886).

THE NOBLE VAGABOND (1886).

HARD HIT (1887).

HEART OF HEARTS (1887).

Performed at the Madison Square Theater, New York 1888.

WEALTH (1889).

Performed at Palmer's Theater, New York 1891.

THE MIDDLEMAN (1889).

Performed, with E. S. Willard, at Palmer's Theater, New York 1890, and on tour.

JUDAH (1890).

Performed, with E. S. Willard, at Palmer's Theater, New York 1891.

SWEET WILL (1890).

Performed at the Standard Theater, New York 1893.

THE DEACON (1890).

Performed at Hoyt's Madison Square Theater, New York 1892.

THE DANCING GIRL (1891).

Performed, with E. H. Sothern, at the Lyceum Theater, New York 1891.

THE CRUSADERS (1891).

THE BAUBLE SHOP (1893).

Performed, with John Drew, at the Empire Theater, New York 1895.

THE TEMPTER (1893).

THE MASQUERADERS (1894).

Performed at the Empire Theater, New York 1895.

THE CASE OF REBELLIOUS SUSAN (1894).

Performed at the Lyceum Theater, New York 1895.

THE TRIUMPH OF THE PHILISTINES (1895).

MICHAEL AND HIS LOST ANGEL (1896).

Performed at the Empire Theater, New York 1896, with Henry Miller and Viola Allen.

THE ROGUE'S COMEDY (1896).

Performed, with E. S. Willard, at Wallack's Theater, New York 1897.

THE PHYSICIAN (1897).

Performed, with E. S. Willard, at Wallack's Theater, New York 1897.

THE LIARS (1897).

Performed, with John Drew, at the Empire Theater, New York 1898.

THE MANŒUVRES OF JANE (1898).

Performed at Daly's Theater, New York 1900.

CARNAC SAHIB (1899).

THE LACKEY'S CARNIVAL (1900).

MRS. DANE'S DEFENCE (1900).

Performed, with Margaret Anglin, at the Empire Theater, New York 1901.

THE PRINCESS'S NOSE (1902).

CHANCE THE IDOL (1902).

WHITEWASHING JULIA (1903).

JOSEPH ENTANGLED (1904).

Performed at the Columbia Theater, San Francisco 1904.

THE CHEVALEER (1904)

THE HEROIC STUBBS (1906).

THE HYPOCRITES (1906).

Performed at the Hudson Theater, New York 1906.

THE GOAL (1907).

Performed at the Princess Theater, New York 1914.

THE EVANGELIST (1907).

Performed at the Knickerbocker Theater, New York 1907.

DOLLY REFORMING HERSELF (1908).

Performed at the Fine Arts Theater, Chicago 1913.

WE CAN'T BE AS BAD AS ALL THAT (1910).

Performed at Nazimova's 39th Street Theater, New York 1910.

THE OGRE (1911).

LYDIA GILMORE (1912).

Performed at the Lyceum Theater, New York 1912.

THE DIVINE GIFT (1912).

MARY GOES FIRST (1913).

Performed, with Marie Tempest, at the Comedy, New York 1914.

THE LIE (1914).

Performed, with Margaret Illington, at the Hudson Theater, New York 1914.

Two or three one-act trifles, together with Jones's and Herman's adaptation of " A Doll's House "—

entitled " Breaking a Butterfly "—are omitted from the above list.

In French's " International Copyrighted Edition " the following plays are published: " Harmony," " Elopement," " Hearts of Oak," " A Clerical Error," " An Old Master," " A Bed of Roses," " The Deacon," and " Sweet Will." In French's special series of Jones's plays are: " Joseph Entangled," " The Silver King," " The Dancing Girl," " The Middleman," " The Hypocrites," " Mrs. Dane's Defence," " The Case of Rebellious Susan," " The Liars," " The Masqueraders," " Dolly Reforming Herself," " The Manœuvres of Jane," " Judah," " The Physician," " The Rogue's Comedy," " The Triumph of the Philistines," " The Crusaders," " Whitewashing Julia," and " The Tempter." Macmillans publish: " Carnac Sahib," " Michael and His Lost Angel," and " Saints and Sinners." " The Divine Gift " and " The Lie " are published by Doran, and " Mary Goes First," by Doubleday, Page (Drama League Series). In " The Theater of Ideas " (Doran) are: " The Goal," " Her Tongue," and " Grace Mary." The other plays are either not published, or else are only privately printed. " Michael and His Lost Angel " is included in " Chief Contemporary Dramatists " (Houghton Mifflin).

REFERENCES: William Archer, " The Theatrical World " (Walter Scott, London), " About the Theater " (Unwin, London), " English Dramatists of To-day " (Sampson Low, London), " Playmaking " (Small, Maynard); Mario Borsa, " The English

Stage of To-day " (Lane); Augustin Filon, " The
English Stage " (Dodd, Mead); George Moore, " Impressions and Opinions" (Brentano); Bernard Shaw,
" Dramatic Opinions and Essays " (Brentano); P. P.
Howe, " Dramatic Portraits " (Kennerley); A. B.
Walkley, " Drama and Life" (Brentano); J. T.
Grein, " Dramatic Criticism" (Evelyn Nash, London); Frank Wadleigh Chandler, " Aspects of Modern Drama " (Macmillan); Clayton Hamilton, " The
Theory of the Theater " and " Studies in Stagecraft "
(Holt); Ludwig Lewisohn, " The Modern Drama "
(Huebsch); Brander Matthews, " A Study of the
Drama " (Houghton Mifflin); introductions to Macmillan (early) editions of " Michael and His Lost
Angel," " The Crusaders," " Saints and Sinners," and
" Judah." By Henry Arthur Jones: " The Renascence of the English Drama " (Macmillan), " The
Foundations of a National Drama " (Doran); introductions to " The Divine Gift," " The Case of Rebellious Susan," and " The Theater of Ideas."—
Magazines: North American, vol. clxxxvi (p. 205);
Reader, vol. ix (p. 105); *Blackwood's,* vol. xciv (p.
283).

THE SILVER KING

A drama in five acts by Henry Arthur Jones and Henry Herman. First performed in 1882.

"The Silver King" was declared by William Archer to be "quite the best of modern English melodramas." Mr. Archer's words have been borne out, if popularity for a period well over a quarter-century be a criterion. Many thousands of performances all over the Continent, in America, South Africa, and Australia, have rendered the play celebrated. This universal appeal rests in the simplicity, sincerity, interest in the plot, and to a certain extent in the sympathetic characters, and above all, in the authors' grasp of the story, and their skill in conducting it from first to last without hesitation. ..

1. Melodrama as distinguished from tragedy is that form of drama in which the story is of more importance than the personages who are in it: the audience will remember the plot, the incidents, the big scenes in "The Silver King" longer than it will the characteristics of Denver. In "Hamlet," on the other hand, it will discuss and ponder over Hamlet's character long after it has forgotten the story and incidents of the Prince of Denmark.

The writer of melodrama invents a frame for his characters, the writer of tragedy will conceive a human being and allow a framework to form itself about him, imposing only such situations as will reveal the inmost soul of that character, and hold the interest of an audience at the same time. Briefly, the hero in tragedy, because he is as he is, brings down the tragedy upon himself, the hero in melodrama merely moves hither and thither until at last the author wills that he fall into the heroine's arms at the final curtain, and the villain be foiled, by fair means or foul.

Distinguish the elements of melodrama in " The Silver King." In exactly what way does the author dictate the actions of the various personages? Are there any elements of true tragedy in the play? Of serious drama—drama in the sense that Pinero's " Iris " is drama?

2. It will be observed that " The Silver King " is divided into seventeen scenes. Why is this? Does it tend to destroy the unity of the acts which are thus divided, or of the entire play? Or is it a confession of weakness on the part of the dramatists?

3. The essential difference between melodrama and tragedy—or a serious play of any kind—is exemplified in the last scene of the first act. Since in the former the dramatist directs the course of events, and the hero follows in their wake, chance

plays an important part; but in the latter, in order
that the audience may believe and eventually see
that the hero's weakness or, it may be, strength,
combined often with external circumstances, causes
his downfall, nothing must be left to chance. His
downfall must seem inevitable. In the third scene
of the first act of " The Silver King " Denver happens to arrive at Ware's home, at the precise
moment when it is being robbed; Ware enters, the
burglar shoots him, after applying the chloroform
pad to Denver, across whose prostrate form he has
stumbled, and the burglars leave. As Denver
awakes to consciousness, he speaks the following
soliloquy:

. . . Where's my hat? (*Gets up, takes candle,
staggers, steadies himself, comes round table, sees
Ware.*) What's that? It's Geoffrey Ware! What's
he doing here? Get up, will you? (*Kneels down.*)
Ah, what's this? Blood! He's shot! My God, I've
murdered him! No! No! Let me think. What
happened? Ah yes, I remember now—I came in
at the door, he sprang at me and then we struggled.
(*Looking at revolver*) My revolver.—One barrel
fired—I've murdered him. No, he's not dead. Geoffrey Ware! Is he dead? (*Eagerly feeling Ware's
pulse*) No, it doesn't beat. (*Tears down Ware's
waistcoat and shirt, puts his ear over Ware's heart.*)
No, no, quite still, quite still. He's dead! Dead!
Dead! Oh, I've killed him—I've killed him. . . .

Although there is a certain poetic justice in the fact that Denver, the drunkard, believes himself to be the murderer of Ware, the various coincidences leading up to this scene, and the fact that Denver's tragedy hinges on a mistake, is too improbable for a serious play—i.e., for any play not a melodrama or a farce. Tragedy demands that there be no accident, no coincidence, to hasten the end of the hero: each event in his downward path must be brought about either through his own fault, or through the implacable laws of fate. Hamlet is the victim of his own weakness, Romeo and Juliet are the victims of fate and circumstances over which they have no control. Denver is the victim of circumstances controlled by the dramatist.

4. Melodrama is a flexible form, yet in its numerous manifestations there are constantly recurring character-types; among these are the villain, hero, and heroine. The villain may be thought of as the force at variance with the hero and the heroine. Before the play reaches the end, the villain must be overpowered through the agency of the hero, who must be united with the heroine. In "The Silver King," who is the hero? The heroine? The villain? What is the struggle between the opposing forces? At what precise point does the decisive struggle take place? How does the hero overcome the villain? Does the heroine help to precipitate the catastrophe?

MICHAEL AND HIS LOST ANGEL

A play in five acts. First performed in 1896.

"Michael and His Lost Angel" is Jones's most
ambitious play. Into it he put his deepest convic-
tions, and succeeded in producing a tragic drama of
passion which may well hold its own with the finest
plays of the time. Bernard Shaw, most catholic of
critics, said of the play: "It seems . . . to me to
be a genuinely sincere and moving play, feelingly
imagined, written with knowledge as to the man and
insight as to the woman by an author equipped not
only with the experience of an adept playwright, and
a kindly and humorous observer's sense of contemporary manners, but with that knowledge of spiritual
history in which Mr. Jones's nearest competitors seem
so stupendously deficient." The play was not a success, owing to difficulties in the original casting, it
was said, but the truth of the matter is expressed in
Shaw's words: "The melancholy truth of the matter
is that the English stage got a good play, and was
completely and ignominiously beaten by it."

1. Measuring "Michael and His Lost Angel"
according to the definitions of tragedy set forth
by Hervieu, and those considered in connection
with "The Silver King" and Pinero's "Iris,"
into what category would this play go?

2. In his "Dramatic Opinions and Essays" (Vol. I, pp. 309-10) Bernard Shaw remarks: "As to the first two acts, I ask nothing better; but at the beginning of the third comes the parting of our ways; and I can point out the exact place where the roads fork. In the first act, Michael, a clergyman, compels a girl who has committed what he believes to be a deadly sin, to confess it publicly in church. In the second act he commits that sin himself. At the beginning of the third act he meets the lady who has been his accomplice; and the following words pass between them:—

Audrie.—You're sorry?
Michael.—No. And you?
Audrie.—No.

Now, after this, what does the clergyman do? Without giving another thought to the all-signifi-cant fact that he is not sorry—that at the very point where, if his code and creed were valid, his conscience would be aching with remorse, he is not only impenitent, but positively glad, he proceeds to act as if he really were penitent, and not only puts on a hair shirt, but actually makes a confession to his congregation in the false character of a con-trite sinner, and goes out from among them with bowed head to exile and disgrace, only waiting in the neighborhood until the church is empty to steal back and privily contradict his pious imposture by picking up and hiding a flower which the woman has thrown on the steps of the altar."

Shaw condemns Michael for not being true to his own conviction: he should either have been sorry, and told Audrie so—in which case there would have been no play—or else not have confessed himself wrong. In the latter case, the play would have been tragic in every sense of the word, for society (external circumstances) would have prevented the couple from living as they thought it right to live, but as it is, we have nothing but a weakling, who is at most a pathetic and not a tragic figure.

How far is Shaw's criticism valid? Does Jones intend Michael to be contrite? Is he really "not sorry," as he declares to Audrie? Is the play a true tragedy?

3. Jones has repeatedly asserted that literature and the drama should be inseparable; a play must stand the test of time, and to do this, it must stand the test of print. In his essay on "Literature and the Modern Drama " * he says: "If your drama is truly alive, it will necessarily be literature." He continues: "If you have faithfully and searchingly studied your fellow-citizens; if you have selected from amongst them those characters that are interesting in themselves, and that also possess an enduring human interest; if in study-

* In "The Foundations of a National Drama" (Doran).

ing these interesting personalities, you have severely selected from the mass of their sayings and doings and impulses, those words and deeds and tendencies which mark them at once as individuals and types; if you have then recast and re-imagined all the materials; if you have cunningly shaped them into a story of progressive and cumulative action; if you have done all this, though you may not have used a single word but what is spoken in ordinary American intercourse to-day, I will venture to say that you have written a piece of live American literature—that is, you have written something that will not only be interesting on the boards of the theater, but can be read with pleasure in your library, can be discussed, argued about, tasted, and digested as literature."

Literature, then, in the drama, is not altogether a matter of style, it concerns itself with arrangement, selection, appropriateness to the characters in the mouths of which words are put, and plot. A play may be written with no pretense to style, and yet be good literature. Certain it is that in the plays of Stephen Phillips the language is finer, the style nearer to perfection than is that of Sardou, yet the Frenchman was a far greater master of *dramatic* literature than the English poet.

In what respects is " Michael and His Lost Angel " literature? Can its style in itself take rank as literature?

THE LIARS

A comedy in four acts. First performed in 1897.

"The Liars" is as fine an example of the comedy of manners in England as any written during the past quarter of a century. The skilful plot-construction, clever dialogue, and genial good-natured satire combine to make it a masterpiece. Behind all the amusement is the eternal "lesson": that society in order to exist must adhere to a set of regulations, and that any infringement of its laws invariably brings social ruin. Needless to say, the idea is not forced upon us; it is allowed, as it should be, to evolve out of the story.

1. In Francis's "Change" (see p. 176), the dramatist eliminates in the third act all the characters except the mother and Lizzie Ann, and concentrates his attention on these two. He does this in order to make of his climax, which occurs at the end of the third act, a unified and striking scene. More than this, he must select from among his characters those to whom the sympathy of the audience is most naturally attracted. An audience must always have its attention directed, as the play approaches its climax, to one person or one small group of persons; or else to one situa-

tion or crisis: when the plot becomes tense there must be no scattering of attention. In Henry Arthur Jones's "Mrs. Dane's Defence" there is a similar narrowing down of the interest, until the climax begins, in the cross-examination scene, where Mrs. Dane and her interlocutor occupy, figuratively as well as actually, the center of the stage. If the action were to be diagrammed it would be represented by a pyramid, the apex of which is the climax.

In "The Liars," the dramatist appears to adopt the reverse method: instead of eliminating characters, he adds to the number from moment to moment. From the very beginning of the third act, he begins building up for the climax. First, the letter from George, which Lady Jessica reads to Lady Rosamund; then Freddie's entrance, adding a further complication; then Sir Christopher's, which seems to promise a way out of the disagreeable predicament; then Mrs. Crispen and Mrs. Coke, and finally George. Most inopportune of all, comes Archibald Coke, who precipitates the final downfall, and not long after, Gilbert, followed by Falkner.

Study in detail the methods by which the cumulative effect is made. If, in "Change" and "Mrs. Dane's Defence," the rise in tension and the elimination of characters can be represented by a pyramid, would not that of "The Liars" be represented by an inverted pyramid? What is the unity of the act?

2. The play is virtually over at the fall of the curtain on the third act. What function does the last fulfil? To what means does the dramatist resort to make the last act interesting? Is it really superfluous?

OSCAR WILDE

Born in Dublin in 1854, of cultured and well-to-do Irish parents, Oscar Wilde spent his early youth in his native country. For three years he attended Trinity College in Dublin, but completed his university education at Oxford, where he devoted himself to classical studies. After traveling in Italy and Greece he came to London. His first book was a volume of poems (1881); these were followed by his first play, " Vera, or the Nihilists," which was performed in the United States in 1883. " The Duchess of Padua," a verse tragedy, was performed in the United States in 1891. Meantime Wilde had been in Paris, there making the acquaintance of many prominent literary men of the period. In 1884 he married, and was enabled thereby, as his wife was a woman of means, to devote his time to lecturing, writing poetry, essays, stories, and plays. The important plays—" Lady Windermere's Fan," " A Woman of No Importance," " An Ideal Husband," and " The Importance of Being Earnest "—were produced between 1892 and 1895. In 1895, Wilde was sentenced to two years' imprisonment with hard labor as the result of a trial instigated by him against the Marquess of Queensberry. (For details of the trial, which are beyond the scope of the present work, see Arthur Ransome's " Oscar Wilde," original edition, and Oscar

Wilde's "De Profundis.") On leaving prison he adopted the name of Sebastian Melmoth and went to France; there, and at Naples, where he later went and wrote "The Ballad of Reading Gaol," he dragged out the few remaining years of his life. He died at Paris in 1900.

In "De Profundis" Wilde said: "I took the drama, the most objective form known to art, and made of it as personal a mode of expression as the lyric or the sonnet; at the same time I widened its range and enriched its characterization." He refers to his "social" plays, and speaks rather of what he intended to do than of actual accomplishment. In his poetic plays and fragments—"The Duchess of Padua," "A Florentine Tragedy," and "Salomé"— he wrote fairly effective pieces and some good pseudo-Elizabethan poetry; in his other plays, with the exception of "Vera," comedies which for their cleverness, their ingenuity, and above all, their wit, are unsurpassed in modern times.

Wilde, more than any other man of his day, recognized the "necessity of style." Although his plays occasionally contain specimens of very artificial and stilted language, still a farce like "The Importance of Being Earnest" is a triumph of literary yet lifelike literature. Wilde was assuredly a man of the theater: he could invent plots and develop an intrigue with extraordinary skill. Henry Arthur Jones, Sir James Barrie, Bernard Shaw, and Granville Barker owe much to their brilliant predecessor.

PLAYS

Vera, or the Nihilists (1883).
   Performed at the Union Square Theater, New York
   1883.
The Duchess of Padua (1891).
   Performed at the Broadway Theater, New York
   1891.
Lady Windermere's Fan (1892).
   Performed at the Columbia Theater, Boston 1893.
A Woman of No Importance (1893).
   Performed at Miner's Fifth Avenue Theater, New
   York 1893.
An Ideal Husband (1895).
   Performed at the Lyceum Theater, New York 1895.
The Importance of Being Earnest (1895).
   Performed at the Empire Theater, New York 1895.
Salomé (1896).
   Performed at the Berkeley Lyceum, New York
   1905.

" La Sainte Courtisane " and " A Florentine Tragedy " are poetic fragments.

Methuen of London publishes the " Chief Works "
of Wilde in twelve volumes. In the United States,
John W. Luce publishes, in four volumes, the " Plays
of Oscar Wilde." Walter H. Baker publishes paper
editions of the " social " plays. In " The Plays of
Oscar Wilde " (Cosmopolitan Edition) published by
H. S. Nichols, all the plays, except the two fragments
above mentioned, are gathered together in a single
volume. " Lady Windermere's Fan " is included in

" Chief Contemporary Dramatists " (Houghton Mifflin).

REFERENCES: Leonard Cresswell Ingleby, " Oscar Wilde " (Werner Laurie, London); Arthur Ransome, " Oscar Wilde " (Kennerley); Lord Alfred Douglas, " Oscar Wilde and Myself " (Lane); Anna, Comtesse de Brémont, " Oscar Wilde and His Mother " (Everett, London); W. W. Kenilworth, " A Study of Oscar Wilde " (Fenno); Holbrook Jackson, " The Eighteen-nineties " (Kennerley); Archibald Henderson, " European Dramatists " (Stewart and Kidd); William Archer, " Playmaking " (Small, Maynard); " The Theatrical World " (Scott, London); Bernard Shaw, " Dramatic Opinions and Essays " (Brentano); Mario Borsa, " The English Stage of To-day " (Lane); Augustin Filon, " The English Stage " (Chapman and Hall, London); C. E. Montague, " Dramatic Values " (Macmillan); F. W. Chandler, " Aspects of Modern Drama " (Macmillan); Ludwig Lewisohn, " The Modern Drama " (Huebsch).—*Magazines: Current Literature*, vol. xxxix (p. 156), vol. xli (p. 518), vol. xliv (p. 287); *Westminster*, vol. clxvi (p. 201); *Arena*, vol. xxxviii (p. 134); *Dial*, vol. xlviii (p. 261); *Bookman*, vol. xxxiv (p. 389); *Nation*, vol. xcviii (pp. 566 and 598), vol. xcix (p. 374).

SALOMÉ

A play in one act. Written in 1892, prohibited in Paris the same year. First produced in that city in 1896. Originally written in French, translated by Lord Alfred Douglas.

"Salomé," like most of Wilde's plays, is a rich and ornate picture: it was written for the purpose of displaying its neat and well-balanced plot, for the sheer pleasure to be derived from its esthetic appeal.* The stage-directions offer the reader something of what is put into the production. The gorgeous and figured style of the dialogue is the work of a poet who plays with words. In the original the style is something of a patch-work: there are many speeches reminiscent of Maeterlinck's early manner, and occasional snatches of Baudelaire and Flaubert. The play is, however, remarkable for its well-handled plot: it is thoroughly dramatic and holds the attention of the audience to the end.†

* The poetic drama in England is discussed in connection with Stephen Phillips's "Paolo and Francesca" (p. 97), as "Salomé" is scarcely a typical example, and is written in a foreign tongue.

† "'In 1901, within a year of the author's death, it was produced in Berlin; from that moment it has held the European stage. It has run for a longer consecutive period in Germany than any play by any Englishman, not excluding Shakespeare. Its popularity has extended

110994

1. As the dramatist in a one-act play cannot afford much space for lengthy and careful exposition, he often sums it up within a few pages or even a few lines. He is forced to concern himself with the play proper. The exposition of " Salomé " is not in the usual form: it is largely the revelation of facts at second-hand, and is done in a more or less summary fashion. The first eight or ten pages are devoted to conversation carried on by the Nubian, the Cappadocian, Herodias's Page, First and Second Soldiers, and the Young Syrian. This is once interrupted by the Voice of Jokanaan. Nowadays we should perhaps regard this sort of exposition as " talky "; it would " retard the action," yet in a poetic play a certain leeway may be allowed for the decorative side of the piece, the inherent beauty of the words, and we are willing to have the atmosphere created, and wait for the entrance of Salomé herself before the story is appreciably advanced.

Compare the opening scene of " Salomé " with the corresponding scenes of Galsworthy's " Strife " and Augustus Thomas's " Arizona."

2. As in most tragedies and in many plays of various kinds, there is a continual insistence of what may be termed the " fate motif." The

to all countries where it is not prohibited. It is performed throughout Europe, Asia, and America. It is played even in Yiddish.'" Quotation from Robert Ross, in Ransome's " Oscar Wilde."

Witches' scenes in " Macbeth " are the classic example. How does Wilde make use of it in this
play?

3. Contrast is a basic principle of all art. In
Richard Strauss's music for the opera of " Salomé," he makes use musically of the interruptions
by Jokanaan, in order to afford a striking contrast to the scene. In the play itself the first in-
terruption—" After me will come another greater
than I," etc.—is a good example of Wilde's use
of contrast. The First Soldier and the Cappadocian have been conversing in short sentences:

First Soldier.—The Jews worship a God they
cannot see.

The Cappadocian.—I cannot understand that.

First Soldier.—Indeed they believe only in those
things they cannot see.

The Cappadocian.—That seems absolutely ridicu-
lous to me.

Then comes the Voice of Jokanaan.—Again:
Salomé speaks of the moon:

Salomé.—How good it is to see the moon! She
resembles a small coin. One might say she was a
little flower of silver. She is cold and chaste, the
moon—I am sure she is a virgin. She has a virgin's
beauty—yes, she is a virgin. She has never soiled
herself. She has never given herself to men, as the
other goddesses have.

The Voice of Jokanaan.—He is come, the Lord!
He is come, the Son of Man. The centaurs have hid
themselves, and the sirens have quitted the streams
and lie under the leaves in the forests.

Notice other examples of dramatic contrast such
as the two above quoted. Is contrast sought by
any other method?

4. Although " Salomé " was not written primarily to be played, it is one of the most effective
of its author's dramatic works. Its success cannot be attributed to the accessory qualities—the
literary style in particular—but rather to its inherent theatrical appeal. Few other one-act plays
move so swiftly, so surely, so rhythmically,
straight up to a climax so well-devised and thrilling as this.

Simplicity is the keynote to the action: from
Salomé's first inquiries about Jokanaan—" Is he
an old man, the prophet? " there is a steady procession of climaxes, or crises, each leading to another and a greater. Salomé's curiosity, then her
strange abnormal love for the uncouth prophet,
Herod's entrance, the momentary pause in the
tension, then the upward flight of the action,
Herod's demand for Salomé to dance, then another moment of suspense, and the rapid climax—
here, in brief, are the qualities, here the unity, the
effectiveness of " Salomé."

LADY WINDERMERE'S FAN

A comedy in four acts. First performed in 1892.

As the form of the play, its wit, its decoration, its pattern " were of more importance to Wilde than the theme or the characters," we may expect that this " play about a good woman " is more a clever excuse for an effective piece of drama and a good deal of verbal pyrotechnics than a sympathetic study of the protagonist. The play has stood the test of time, because it is a good story—in spite of its flagrant shortcomings—so that there is no need of discussing its sincerity of purpose.

1. The first act—in the earlier version—ends with the following speech of Lord Windermere:

(*Calling after her.*) Margaret! Margaret! (*A pause*) My God! What shall I do? I dare not tell her who this woman really is. The shame would kill her. (*Sinks down into a chair and buries his face in his hands.*)

In later editions the speech is altered to:

My God! What shall I do? I dare not tell her that this woman is her mother!

Why was the change made? How does it affect

the attitude of the audience in the succeeding acts?

2. It is perhaps unjust to criticise this play as a serious comment on life, one in which we must believe and feel for the characters, yet some of the more important weak points must not be left unnoticed. Some pages from the end of the first act, Lady Windermere speaks the following lines:

How horrible! I understand now what Lord Darlington meant by the imaginary instance of the couple not two years married. Oh! It can't be true —she spoke of enormous sums of money paid to this woman. I know where Arthur keeps his bank book —in one of the drawers of that desk. I might find out by that. I *will* find out. (*Opens drawer.*) No, it is some hideous mistake. (*Rises and goes C.*) Some silly scandal! He loves *me!* He loves *me!* But why should I not look? I am his wife, I have a right to look! (*Returns to bureau, takes out book and examines it, page by page, smiles and gives a sigh of relief.*) I knew it, there is not a word of truth in this stupid story. (*Puts book back in drawer. As she does so, starts and takes out another book.*) A second book—private—locked! (*Tries to open it, but fails. Sees paper knife on bureau, and with it cuts cover from book. Begins to start at the first page.*) Mrs. Erlynne—600—Mrs. Erlynne—700 —Mrs. Erlynne—400. Oh! it is true! it is true! How horrible! (*Throws book on floor.*)

(*Enter Lord Windermere, C.*)

The dramatic effect is too easily achieved, it is too obvious, and in consequence a little discrimination will prevent our believing what we see. The improbability of the situation is too apparent. Further, Lord Windermere's giving Mrs. Erlynne the money, his poor excuse that " the shame would kill her " (Lady Windermere) are insufficient motives. Had Wilde really cared to make his audience believe, he would not have made as the basis of the rest of the play so insecure a foundation. But he was concerned chiefly with externals ; he knew that he was telling an interesting, if improbable story, he had numerous choice epigrams and some effective dramatic material for the ensuing acts—and besides, had Lord Windermere told Lady Windermere the truth, there would have been no play!

The fundamental mistake just pointed out in the first act weakens the ensuing action, and Lord Windermere's secret results in his wife's attempted elopement with Lord Darlington. There is no need multiplying instances of the like, for as the plot proceeds, the weak motivation becomes more and more apparent. By the time the " big " scene comes, with its heavy tirade, we doubt the sincerity of the characters. The " Believe what you choose about me " speech in the third act fails to ring true.

3. Wilde's skill in preparing for an effective

scene has been already observed in " Salomé." In
" The Importance of Being Earnest " there is an
even better example. What instances are there in
the present play?

THE IMPORTANCE OF BEING EARNEST

A " Trivial Comedy for Serious People "; a farce in
three acts. First performed in 1895.

A farce is a comic play in which the audience is
asked to accept impossible or highly improbable situations for the time being. It differs radically from
comedy, in that the audience must believe, for if the
personages are to appear real—and they must, as
character is of prime importance in comedy—they
must move about in real situations, or at least such
as we can give credence to. In a farce, then, what
the characters *do* is of more importance than what
they *are*. " The Importance of Being Earnest " is a
farce, one of the best ever written, cleverly constructed and delightfully amusing. There is only the
slightest attempt at the sketching of character, while
most of the personages are at best but caricatures; the
author's skill is brought to bear chiefly upon the situations and the lines. It so happens that this farce
contains more clever lines, puns, epigrams, and deft
repartees than any other of modern times, but these
are after all accessory. A farce may be written without these additions—it might well be pure pantomime.
Wilde has thrown them in for full measure.

1. The first act should be carefully studied after
a reading of the entire play. Notice especially

how the very comic scene in the second act—where
Jack enters " in the deepest mourning "—is prepared for and led up to. In order that this scene
shall be a surprise, and that the appearance of
Jack, without a spoken word, shall evoke a series
of recognitions in the mind of the audience, and
a correlation of hitherto-unknown facts, the preparation in the first act must be skilfully done.
The very casualness and apparent triviality of the
dialogue tend to throw us off our guard. This is
in a manner comparable with the art of the magi-
cian who, while calling attention to a dexterous
feat of legerdemain with his right hand, prepares
the next trick with his left. So, in the first act,
we are scarcely aware of the importance of
Algernon's disquisition on " Bunburying," or of
Algernon's writing the address which Jack gives to
Gwendolyn " on his shirt-cuff," so nonchalantly
are these points introduced. Yet, when the scene
in question—in Act II—comes, we are perfectly
acquainted with the necessary facts.

2. That farce can be independent of clever
dialogue is, as we have said, true, but when this
can be added and made to fit into the action and
further it, so much the better for farce. Oscar
Wilde could not resist the temptation to be witty,
though this practice was often detrimental to the
rest of the work. In " Lady Windermere's Fan,"
indeed, the wit covers occasional bungling in the

plot. But in " The Importance of Being Earnest," Wilde found a form which he could make " personal," and plot and wit go hand in hand. Take, for instance, the following dialogue from the first act:

Algernon.—Well, my dear fellow, you need not eat as if you were going to eat it all. You behave as if you were married to her already. You are not married to her already, and I don't think you ever will be.

Jack.—Why on earth do you say that?

Algernon.—Well, in the first place, girls never marry the men they flirt with. Girls don't think it right.

Jack.—Oh, that is nonsense.

Algernon.—It isn't. It is a great truth. It accounts for the extraordinary number of bachelors that one sees all over the place. In the second place, I don't give my consent.

The epigram is not forced, as many epigrams are forced in the first act of " A Woman of No Importance "; it is in keeping with the characters and situation. At the same time it serves the ends of drama, by advancing the story and affording some insight into the character of the personages.

Find other examples of this in the present play.

3. The third act of a farce—and it is extremely dangerous to extend a farce to more than three

acts—is unusually difficult. The effort to maintain interest for two acts often leaves a dramatist exhausted by the time he comes to conclude.

How well has Wilde succeeded in accumulating his interest in the third act of this play? Has he relied upon the wit of the lines, or has he carefully brought together the threads of action and given sufficient *raison d'être* to his summing up? Compare the third act of " The Importance of Being Earnest " with the fourth of " Lady Windermere's Fan." Which is the better, and why?

BERNARD SHAW

George Bernard Shaw was born in Dublin in 1856. From the son's own account, the father must have been a rather shiftless and unimaginative man, but his mother—who was to exert great influence over the boy—was a woman of culture. The family, when George Bernard was a youth, found itself in reduced circumstances, and the son was forced to enter a land-agent's office in his native city. He was always interested in music (this taste he received from his mother) and science, and in the confinement of office life he gave early signs of his restless and revolutionary character. In 1876 he went to London. For nine years he did literary hack-work, living in a shabby room on next to nothing. His efforts were long unrecognized, and he had to accept a small pit-. tance for some years from his mother. Four novels— "The Irrational Knot," "Love Among the Artists," "The Unsocial Socialist," and "Cashel Byron's Profession"—were written between 1880 and 1883, but they brought their author neither fame nor prosperity. He was not, however, wasting his time, for his association with small clubs and societies—atheistical and socialistic in tendency—brought him into contact with a number of influential men. Among these was Sidney Webb, the economist. Waxing enthusiastic over the ideas of Henry George, he began to take active interest in the problems of poverty, and joined the

Land Reform Union. For some years Shaw attended
lectures, studied Socialism, Trade Unionism, and
kindred subjects, and made friends with Edward Carpenter and William Morris. He made the acquaintance, too, of William Archer, in 1885, and was
induced to enter the field of newspaper criticism.
Before long, he fulfilled the functions, in turn, of
musical, art, and dramatic critic. As dramatic critic
of the *Saturday Review*, he exercised widespread influence, as champion of Ibsen and the new ideas of
dramatic writing, and enemy of the out-worn conventions so long accepted by the theater-world. Meantime he had been busy with propaganda work in connection with the Fabian Society, and delivered numerous lectures on economic and political questions. In
1892 his first play, "Widowers' Houses," was produced at J. T. Grein's then recently-established Independent Theater. Then followed "The Philanderer"
(1893), and "Mrs. Warren's Profession," which
was censored and not produced until 1902. By this
time Shaw had come to be considered a new force in
the theater, but success, in the usual sense of the term,
did not come to him for many years. Such organiza-
tions as the Stage Society and the Court Theater—
where Granville Barker produced play after play of
Shaw—did most to bring him to the knowledge of
the public at large, a knowledge acquired in Germany
some years before. Shaw has been engaged in many
branches of work, but his activity has not been limited to books and plays. He is at the same time an
eloquent speaker, economist, and great-spirited citizen.

In his first volume of the " Plays Pleasant and Unpleasant," Bernard Shaw said that, having had his eyesight tested by a specialist, he was informed that he was " an exceptional and highly fortunate being, optically, normal sight conferring the power of seeing things accurately, and being enjoyed by only about ten per cent. of the population, the remaining ninety per cent. being abnormal." Coming as he did, when Pinero and Jones were endeavoring to produce new and original works, albeit in the old forms, Shaw with his normal eyesight began looking about him and discovered that there were new things to say in new ways, and he said them in a manner which at first startled the " ninety per cent." In other words, his early attempts—like " Widowers' Houses " and " Mrs. Warren's Profession "—were advance-guard works, aimed primarily at those dramatists who still clung to the drawing-room type of play and the ideas that more often than not accompanied it. In the preface to the volume above referred to he says: " Finally, a word as to why I have labeled the three plays in this first volume Unpleasant. The reason is pretty obvious: their dramatic power is used to force the spectator to face unpleasant facts. No doubt all plays which deal sincerely with humanity must wound the monstrous conceit which it is the business of romance to flatter." All of Shaw's early plays and most of his later ones were protests against the conventions, the lifelessness, the timidity of the play of the day. This he did as a dramatist; as a commentator on life, it is more difficult to determine just what he has done.

Shaw considers himself a Socialist and intellectual leader who chooses to employ the stage as the best means of promulgating his ideas. Until recently, at least, he has proclaimed himself not a dramatist but a preacher. Yet, in the final analysis, Shaw will be remembered as a remarkably clever and gifted dramatist with an unusual endowment of wit and considerable ability to tell a good story. His best plays—" Candida," " Arms and the Man," " Man and Superman "—are occasionally marred as dramas by too much irrelevant " talk." Yet that talk is so amusing, so interesting, so witty, and so pregnant with ideas, that it is difficult to criticise the work as a whole. Shaw has at least proved that a good play can contain a vast amount of conversation and very little action.

Shaw, in company with Jones and Pinero and Wilde, is one of the founders of modern English drama. As dramatic critic, lecturer, and dramatist, his influence has been probably the deepest and most widespread of any of his contemporaries.

PLAYS

WIDOWERS' HOUSES (1892).

THE PHILANDERER (1893).

Performed at the Little Theater, Chicago 1914.

MRS. WARREN'S PROFESSION (1893).*

Performed at the Hyperion Theater, New Haven 1905; Garrick Theater, New York, same year.

ARMS AND THE MAN (1894).

Performed, with Richard Mansfield, Herald Square Theater, New York 1894.

* Produced in 1902.

CANDIDA (1897).

Performed at the Princess Theater, New York
1903.

THE MAN OF DESTINY (1897).

Performed at the American Academy, New York
1899.

YOU NEVER CAN TELL (1900).

Performed at the Garrick Theater, New York 1905.

THE DEVIL'S DISCIPLE (1899).

Performed at Bleeker Hall, Albany 1897.

CÆSAR AND CLEOPATRA (1899).

Performed at the New Amsterdam Theater, New
York 1906.

CAPTAIN BRASSBOUND'S CONVERSION (1900).

Performed, with Ellen Terry, Empire Theater,
New York 1907.

MAN AND SUPERMAN (1905).

Performed, with Robert Lorraine, Hudson Theater,
New York 1905.

JOHN BULL'S OTHER ISLAND (1904).

Performed at the Garrick Theater, New York 1905.

HOW HE LIED TO HER HUSBAND (1905).

Performed at the Berkeley Lyceum, New York
1904.

MAJOR BARBARA (1905).

THE DOCTOR'S DILEMMA (1906).

Performed at Wallack's Theater, New York 1915.

GETTING MARRIED (1908).

THE SHEWING-UP OF BLANCO POSNET (1909).

Performed by the Irish Players in several cities of
the United States 1911-2.

MISALLIANCE (1910).

THE DARK LADY OF THE SONNETS (1910).

FANNY'S FIRST PLAY (1911).

    Performed at Collier's Comedy Theater, New York 1912.

ANDROCLES AND THE LION (1913).

    Performed at Wallack's Theater, New York 1915.

PYGMALION (1913).

    Performed, with Mrs. Patrick Campbell, Park Theater, New York 1914.

GREAT CATHERINE (1914).

(This list follows the order of publication. Owing to difficulties with the censorship and of obtaining suitable companies for production, some of the plays were performed in England some time after they had appeared in the United States.)

Besides the above-mentioned plays a few topical sketches and occasional pieces should be mentioned: " Passion, Poison, and Petrifaction " (1905); " The Interlude at the Playhouse " (1907); " The Admirable Bashville " (1903); " Press Cuttings " (1909); " Overruled " (1912); and " The Music Cure " (1914).

The first three and the next four plays are published in " Plays Pleasant and Unpleasant " (Brentano); the next three in " Three Plays for Puritans " (Brentano); " Man and Superman " separately (Brentano); the next three under their own titles (Brentano); likewise with the next two groups of three; " Androcles and the Lion," " Pygmalion," and " Great Catherine " appeared in *Everybody's Maga-*

zine (September and November, 1914, and February, 1915). "The Admirable Bashville" and "Press Cuttings" are published separately (Brentano); "Overruled" in *The English Review* (May, 1913). The others, with the exception of "The Music Cure," appeared respectively in magazines and newspapers which to-day are unobtainable.

Brentano's publish in separate paper editions most of the plays above listed.

REFERENCES: G. K. Chesterton, "George Bernard Shaw" (Lane); Archibald Henderson, "George Bernard Shaw, His Life and Works" (Stewart and Kidd); Holbrook Jackson, "Bernard Shaw, A Study and an Appreciation" (Richards); Henry L. Mencken, "George Bernard Shaw, His Plays" (Luce); Joseph McCabe, "George Bernard Shaw" (Kennerley); Renee M. Deacon, "Bernard Shaw as Artist-Philosopher" (Lane); William Archer, "The Theatrical World" (Walter Scott, London), "Playmaking" (Small, Maynard); Mario Borsa, "The English Stage of To-day" (Lane); Augustin Filon, "The English Stage" (Dodd, Mead); Ashley Dukes, "Modern Dramatists" (Sergel); E. E. Hale, Jr., "Dramatists of To-day" (Holt); Archibald Henderson, "European Dramatists" (Stewart and Kidd), "The Changing Drama" (Holt); P. P. Howe, "Dramatic Portraits" (Kennerley); James Huneker, "Iconoclasts" (Scribner); J. M. Kennedy, "English Literature, 1880-1905" (Stephen Swift, London); C. E. Montague, "Dramatic Values" (Macmillan); D. E. Oliver, "The English Stage" (Ousley,

London); John Jay Chapman, " Memories and Mile-
stones " (Moffat, Yard); Gilbert Norwood, " Eurip-
ides and Mr. Bernard Shaw " (St. Catherine Press,
London); H. M. Walbrook, " Nights at the Play "
(Ham-Smith, London); A. B. Walkley, " Drama and
Life " (Brentano), " Frames of Mind " (Richards,
London); John Palmer, " The Future of the Theater "
(Bell, London), " The Censor and the Theaters "
(Kennerley), " George Bernard Shaw: Harlequin or
Patriot? " (Century Co.); W. L. George, " Dramatic
Actualities " (Sidgwick and Jackson, London); Cecil
F. Armstrong, " From Shakespeare to Shaw " (Mills
and Boon, London); Frank Wadleigh Chandler,
" Aspects of Modern Drama " (Macmillan); Ludwig
Lewisohn, " The Modern Drama " (Huebsch).—
Magazines: Independent, vol. lix (p. 1060); *Fort-
nightly,* vol. lxxxv (p. 516); *North American,* vol.
clxxx (p. 746); *Bookman,* vol. xxi (p. 428), vol. xxvii
(p. 474); *Poet-Lore,* Sept.-Oct., 1909; *Arena,* vol.
xxxii (p. 489); *Atlantic,* vol. ciii (p. 227); *Current
Literature,* vol. xxxix (p. 551); *Cosmopolitan,* vol. xl
(p. 339); *Contemporary,* vol. cxiii (p. 422); *Academy,*
vol. lx (p. 192); *Edinburgh Review,* vol. cci (p. 498);
Hibbert Journal, vol. viii (p. 818); *Outlook,* vol. lxxxi
(p. 701); *Drama,* No. 12.

CANDIDA

A mystery in three acts. First performed in 1897.

"Candida" is a shaft aimed against current conceptions of what is moral, right, and fitting. It has always been accepted as a commonplace that the father is the respected head of the family, yet Crampton in "You Never Can Tell" shows that all fathers are not and should not be such; "Man and Superman" attempts to prove that in the eternal question of sex-mating, it is the woman and not the man who gives chase and brings down her prey. In "Candida" Shaw shatters ideals about the "sanctity of the family," and shows a weak man and a strong man —each at first appearing to be the reverse—with a woman between them. The woman finally clings to the weaker, as he needs her most; not, Shaw implies, because she happens to be his wife.

"Candida" is among its author's best plays. As an acting piece it is certainly his best. Not radically different from the "well-made play" it takes the old conventions and turns them into new channels, and promulgates ideas which are for the most part strictly germane to the story, sets forth characters with vividness, in a highly entertaining way. Shaw had not as yet freed himself from those elements of "Sardoodledom" against which he had so vigorously protested in his early days as a critic. As will be seen,

" Man and Superman " was a great advance stride toward technical freedom, while " Getting Married " and " Misalliance " at length bridged the gap.

1. The plays of the past fifty years differ strikingly from those of earlier times as regards the matter of stage-directions. The Greeks, the Latins, and the Elizabethans wrote primarily for the simplest of stages, so that the merest suggestion (Entrances, Exits, and so on) sufficed for the manager. There are few indications of " business." Since it has become the custom to issue plays in book form, many dramatists feel the need of amplifying and expounding. Ibsen was among the first to do this, and Shaw has followed in his steps. With the development of the drama, which has been extraordinarily rapid since Ibsen's day, has come the need of commenting upon the more complex settings and subtler characters, which are comparatively new. In general, the earlier plays were simpler, they treated characters more as types, than nowadays. With the advent of Ibsen, stock actors found that " First Lead," " Villain," and " Ingénue " were not sufficient. Therefore Ibsen told something about his characters in stage-directions. Not satisfied with this, Shaw told a great deal.* He carried the practice almost to an

* " It is astonishing to me," says Shaw in his preface to " Plays Pleasant and Unpleasant," Vol. I, that Ibsen, who devotes two years to the production of a three-act play,

extreme, but he was practically forced to do so, because his early plays were either censored or badly cast, or were for other reasons not successful on the stage.

Determine, after a careful reading of the stage-directions in this play, which among them can be utilized by the actor, manager, and stage-carpenter, and which are for the reader alone.

Compare the stage-directions of Granville Barker in a play like " The Voysey Inheritance " or " The Madras House," and of Barrie in " The Twelve-pound Look," with those of " Candida."

2. Among the most persistent of the many criticisms urged against Shaw is that the characters in his plays are for the most part merely puppets, without life and emotions, set in action by a very clever thinker and craftsman. In his " Dramatic Portraits," P. P. Howe states of the characters in " Mrs. Warren's Profession," and makes the

the extraordinary quality of which depends on a mastery of characterization and situation which can only be achieved by working out a good deal of the family and personal history of the individuals represented, should nevertheless give the reading public very little more than the technical memorandum required by the carpenter, the gasman, and the prompter. Who will deny that the resultant occasional mysteriousness of effect, enchanting though it may be, is produced at the cost of intellectual obscurity? Ibsen, interrogated as to his meaning, replies, 'What I have said I have said.' Precisely, but the point is that what he hasn't said he hasn't said."

remark applicable to Shaw's characters in general:
" . . . They are puppets at the end of wires, and
the wires are attached to a battery, and Mr. Shaw
is in charge of the current." Usually, Shaw is so
much in earnest, so " full of his message," that he
cannot adopt the aloof attitude as, for instance,
Galsworthy does—and allow his personages to
speak and act in accordance with their own
thoughts, passions, and beliefs. Still, how far
does Mr. Howe's criticism apply to " Candida "?
To Lady Cecily Waynfleete in " Captain Brassbound's Conversion "? Dick Dudgeon in " The
Devil's Disciple "? Are these people human beings, or are they only puppets?

3. Shaw spoke of the occasional mysteriousness
in Ibsen's plays resulting from a lack of proper
stage-directions. What is the value of Shaw's
own stage-directions in " Candida "? Especially
in the latter part of the first act? Would that
scene between Marchbanks and Morrell be quite
intelligible without them? Could the dramatist
have made it so without them? Has he failed,
using the novelist's method in default of dramatic
dialogue?—What, at the end of the final act, was
" The secret in the poet's heart "?

4. During his early and confessedly propagandist days Bernard Shaw fulminated against the
conventions of the " well-made " play; and yet he
not infrequently made use of those same conven-

tions in his own plays. As one critic put it, he fell in love with his own medium, and it finally mastered him.

In " Candida " determine in what respects the play is " well-made." Are the " curtains " effective? What of the exposition? Is it clever? Obvious? And the development? Compare this play, as to its structure, with Sudermann's " Magda " and Björnson's " Leonarda."

(A still more " old-fashioned " play of Shaw's is his first, " Widowers' Houses." Notice the " asides," the soliloquy, and the numerous stilted speeches in that play.)

MAN AND SUPERMAN

A comedy and a philosophy; a play in four acts.
First performed in 1905.

We have seen how in the best of Shaw's work up
to the production of " Man and Superman " the
thinker and preacher, while eternally trying to assert
himself, was somehow subordinated to the dramatist.
In this comedy—and a philosophy—however, the play
itself is used only as a framework for a thesis. In
the preface to the popular edition the author wrote:
" As I have not been sparing of such lighter qualities
as I could endow the book with for the sake of those
who ask nothing from a play but agreeable pastime,
I think it well to affirm plainly that the third act,
however fantastic its legendary framework may appear, is a careful attempt to write a new Book of
Genesis for the Bible of the Evolutionists. . . ."
Not content with a long prefatory letter, he added a
seventy-five-page " Revolutionist's Handbook " to his
190-page play, in order to expound what of his
philosophy he was unable to crowd into the incidental
comedy.

As a brilliant achievement, an amusing collection of
pamphlets, as a piece of sustained clear thinking, the
volume is a noteworthy achievement, yet " Man and
Superman," as a play in the ordinary sense of the
word, comes near to being spoiled: there is so much

dissertation and so vast a sermon, that the play—
what there is of action and character—occasionally
appears as an impertinent intrusion. Still, there is
enough left when it is presented—minus the third act,
which has never been played with the rest—to allow
one to see how good it might have been.

1. In his everlasting protest against the " in-
corribly romantic " Englishman, Shaw has written
good plays according to the old dramatic formulas,
and equally good ones after he threw them aside.
In his splendid revolt against all that he considers
false in art and life he has been consistent. Still,
his contribution has been for the most part a negative one. In " Arms and the Man " his message
was the destruction of the conventional and
" heroic " soldier; in " Widowers' Houses " he
made of Blanche a cold and unsympathetic girl,
largely because he felt that Pinero and G. R.
Sims would have made her a little friend of the
poor. And so, in " Man and Superman " the love-
scenes are reversed, as it were: the aggressive Ann
Whitefield pursues the unwilling Jack Tanner.
The conventional dramatists of all times have pic-
tured the lover at the feet of his mistress, who is
usually haughty and distant. Not content with
telling the mere truth, and unwilling to utter half-
truths about poverty and war and sex, Shaw has
stated what appears to his normal eyes as the rule,
from what seems to the average reader and play-

goer a decidedly oblique angle. This he has done
for the sake of emphasis.

Shaw's "love-scenes" are highly characteristic
of his dramatic methods. Take the lovers in
"Widowers' Houses," those in "Mrs. Warren's
Profession," "Arms and the Man," "You Never
Can Tell," "The Doctor's Dilemma," and "Pygmalion"; compare them with the lovers in Pinero's
"Iris," Jones's "Michael and His Lost Angel,"
and Edward Sheldon's "Romance." As a rule,
Shaw is mortally afraid of anything touching
upon the romantic—yet in "Candida," "The
Doctor's Dilemma," and "The Shewing-up of
Blanco Posnet," he indulges in his own peculiar
way in the universal failing. He never approaches
the Latin method, where lovers express in words
and gestures every breath in the whirlwind of passion. It should not be too hastily concluded that
Shaw is averse from the depiction of true passion
—Mrs. Dubedat in "The Doctor's Dilemma" is
intended as a deep-feeling woman—but rather that
he was dissatisfied with the conventional treatment
which too often masqueraded as such, and not that
he was, in the words of Vaughn in his own
"Fanny's First Play," "psychologically incapable
of the note of passion." Shaw is too much an
artist not at least to try to make use of such powers
as he possesses.

2. The first act is as good a first act as Shaw

ever wrote: there is little discursiveness, the plot is carefully, amusingly, and interestingly, begun. But is it quite clear? Is, for instance, the mistake as to Violet's position—the scene occupying the last few pages of the act—made unmistakably plain? The act closes on this scene, and great importance is assumed as belonging to the episode. Technique or no technique, the end of an act is a conspicuous place, and what is put there is bound to attract attention.

3. The second act is on the whole good drama, concerned for the most part with the Ann-Tanner story; it progresses straight up to the little climax. The starting of the motor, visible to the audience, is a clever device for thrusting the plot forward. Straker is possibly a little puzzling, but he is so amusing that we may excuse his dramatic " superfluity." So far, then, so good.

4. The third act is never played—except independently, as " Don Juan in Hell "—the reason given being that the entire play would prove too long for a single representation. But Bernard Shaw is always so scrupulous and uncompromising in the matter of the presentation of his plays, that this excuse must be taken as tantamount to a confession of failure: the act is practically negligible so far as the play itself is concerned. Fortunately, there was scarcely any preparation in the two preceding acts for this act, nor does the third contain

much that concerns the fourth. Only a very few minor changes are made for the stage version.

Read the third act, and try to determine what relation it has with the rest of the play.

5. The last act is good and bad, dramatically. In nearly every play of Shaw the dramatic qualities should be carefully differentiated from the intellectual, the didactic, the intrinsically amusing. The earlier pages of this fourth act are interesting and amusing, but Malone's talk about Ireland properly belongs to " John Bull's Other Island." " Man and Superman " is only resumed when Tanner and Ann take the stage again, and Ann, summoning up all her power in order to fulfil her mission in regard to the " Life Force," finally captures Tanner.

Some of the more striking difficulties under which the dramatist labored in trying to weld together many utterly foreign elements in this play have been touched upon in this outline. Can you discover others? There is little need to indicate the redeeming features of " Man and Superman ": the intellectual agility, the wit, the good humor, the essential truth of the ideas set forth. These are evident, but only because Shaw is so nearly a great dramatist is it worth the student's while to observe his shortcomings.

GETTING MARRIED

A comedy in one scene. First performed in 1908.

If Bernard Shaw's plays are considered in chronological order, from "Widowers' Houses" to "Misalliance," it will be observed that they evolve, as regards their technical form, from what is a more or less close approximation to the old-fashioned well-made play to the loosest sort of conversation play. In studying the two plays already outlined, we have seen how "Candida" was in many respects "well-made," and how "Man and Superman" departed to a great extent from formulas. In "Getting Married" a radical departure will be observed; a complete neglect of technical canons. The author claims to have returned to the Greek Unities, but this must be considered rather the result of coincidence than of conscious effort.

1. Nowadays it is more difficult to classify plays than formerly: there are comedies which end with the death of the principal character (Rostand's "Cyrano de Bergerac" and Jules Lemaître's "Bertrade"), nondescript pieces in which the hero dies and his wife remarries (Shaw's "The Doctor's Dilemma"), and others which defy classification (Andreyeff's "Anathema" and Wedekind's "Such

is Life "). For example, the term " play of ideas "
may be applied to many of Ibsen's later works,
yet " The Wild Duck " and " Rosmersholm "
are much more than this. Tchekoff's " The Sea-
gull " is certainly a play of ideas, but it is at the
same time a comedy of conversation and a tragedy.
Yet, if we attempt to narrow the term, we may in
general call most of Brieux's plays, most of
Hervieu's, all of Paul-Hyacinthe Loyson's,*
many of Shaw's, and some of Galsworthy's, plays
of ideas.† It has already been pointed out that
every good play must be based upon some idea,
but the particular kind of play to which we now
refer is that in which the dramatist's prime purpose is to furnish, discuss, and evolve ideas. In
this sense, then, " Getting Married " is a play of
ideas.

The form is not fixed, yet one of its characteristics is a good deal of conversation: the easiest
and, in many cases, most direct method of convey-
ing ideas on the stage is through the medium of
dialogue. Yet the moment an audience is required to listen to talk, the talk must be super-
latively interesting or otherwise attractive, for ac-

* " Les Ames ennemies," " L'Evangile du sang," and
" L'Apôtre." (The last-named is translated by Barrett H.
Clark as " The Apostle," in The Drama League Series.)
† Brieux's " Damaged Goods " (" Les Avariés "), Her-
vieu's " La Loi de l'homme," and Galsworthy's " Justice,"
are plays of ideas.

tion is necessarily lacking. But Shaw is a consummate dialectician and a master of speech. Were it not for this extraordinary cleverness and the sheer interest aroused by the discussion, " Getting Married " would be a very dull pamphlet. Nothing occurs; a group of interesting characters sit around and talk.

2. In the introductory note to the printed edition of the play, the author says: " N.B. There is a point of some technical interest to be noted in this play. The customary division into acts and scenes has been disused, and a return made to unity of time and place as observed in the ancient Greek drama. In 'The Doctor's Dilemma,' there are five acts; the place is altered five times; and the time is spread over an undetermined period of more than a year. No doubt the strain on the attention of the audience and on the ingenuity of the playwright is much less; but I find in practice that the Greek form is inevitable when drama reaches a certain point in poetic and intellectual evolution. Its adoption was not, on my part, a deliberate display of virtuosity in form, but simply the spontaneous falling of a play of ideas into the form most suitable to it, which turned out to be the classical form. 'Getting Married,' in several acts and scenes, with the time spread over a long period, would be impossible."

Notice, however, that Shaw does not claim unity

of action, the third of Aristotle's Unities, for the very good reason that there is no action to unify.

3. With the above explanation as a basis, and with what of the long preface the reader cares to peruse, let him see how the dramatist has managed to present his characters and his ideas so as to interest his audience.

First, the theme is of interest to the greater part of the audience; second, a large number and variety of characters is introduced; third, the details, the odds and ends of what would be action in an ordinary play, are allowed especial prominence.

In what other ways does Shaw attract and hold the attention? What are his methods for supplying an equivalent of action, story, suspense, etc.?

4. Once again, is it pertinent to inquire, What is a Play? (See Introduction to " The Continental Drama of To-day.") Critics find it needful to modify their definitions, if they are sufficiently courageous to make them, so that it might not be a great exaggeration to declare that anything that " goes " on the stage is a play.

After all, is there any basis for the assertion that because " Getting Married " has no action, it is therefore merely a series of dialogues on marriage? Has not Shaw rather helped to broaden the field of drama?

5. In what respects, if any, is this " comedy "

a play, in the accepted conventional sense of the term? Are there any resemblances here to a work like "The Second Mrs. Tanqueray," or "Magda"?

6. Do you see any reason why Shaw, after writing "Getting Married" and "Misalliance," returned to the more conventional forms in "The Shewing-up of Blanco Posnet," "Fanny's First Play," and "Pygmalion"?

THE SHEWING-UP OF BLANCO POSNET

A play in one act. First produced in 1909. (Censored in England.)

This "crude sermon in melodrama" is one of the most pointedly didactic of all Shaw's plays. As there is scarcely enough material to warrant its development into two or three acts, the author rightly puts it into one. Yet as it now stands it is not a highly successful one-act play. Sudermann's "Fritzchen" contains but a single incident, which is treated in one breath, as it were: the audience is present while the tragedy is enacted. In Shaw's play, however, the audience sees only sections of the play, rather disjointed sections. Sudermann was interested primarily in the artistic effect, Shaw in the demonstration of a psychological and religious phenomenon. When it is possible to set forth an idea and do it artistically, Shaw is willing to be an artist, but when the idea must suffer, Shaw prefers to be less an artist and more a preacher.

1. As the audience for which the dramatist originally wrote was unacquainted with the *milieu* —as was Shaw himself—he was forced to create it: notice the rather pointed conversation among the women which occupies the first four pages. These speeches acquaint us with the situation, and

prepare us for Blanco's entrance (p. 411). Again, the stage-directions accomplish much more than Blanco's words, because Shaw could more easily describe a character of whom he had no first-hand knowledge than make him real by means of speech and action.

Possibly the occasional stilted and foreign atmosphere throughout is due to the fact that the entire setting and characters are drawn from the dramatist's knowledge of Bret Harte and Jack London, rather than Blanco Posnet himself and Elder Daniels.

2. On the bottom of page 414 begins a long conversation between Blanco and his brother. This dialogue is introduced for the purpose of making clear something of the lives of the two men: the six pages advance the theme while the play, as drama, stands still. The artistic unity of the piece suffers, while Shaw accomplished his end. The action is resumed the moment (p. 421) Strapper says, " I've got my witness; and I'll trouble you not to make a move towards her when she comes in to identify you." The woman Blanco expects does not come in; this time it is only Feemy, but the audience, seeing Blanco's fear, is curious to know the exact reason. He is not afraid of Feemy, that is certain. Who, then, is the mysterious woman of whom the horse-thief said: " A woman? She ain't real: neither is the child." The trial

then proceeds. This is a good scene, full of amusing and character-revealing incidents. Then (p. 433) the action stops, and The Woman enters. Up to this point the dramatist has been preparing the scene for the statement of his thesis. Blanco, having undergone his one great " religious experience," now begins to show the results of it.

The Sheriff.—Where's the child?

Strapper.—On Pug Johnson's bench in his shed. He's making a coffin for it.

Blanco.—(*with a horrible convulsion of the throat, frantically*) Dead! The little Judas kid! The child I gave my life for! (*He breaks into hideous laughter.*)

It is dangerous to stop the action of a play, especially a one-act play, within a few minutes of the end, but in this case the thesis is so interesting and the action so relatively unimportant, that the audience is likely to forget the play for the idea.

3. The thesis of this play is so abstract, so subtle, that the dramatist must resort to extremes, to " get it over." It is more than likely that such a man as the hardened horse-thief would have said nothing of the revolution which had taken place in his soul, had it not been for the entrance of The Woman. This was Shaw's method of showing, not the experience itself—which would have been impossible—but the result of the experience. But in

order to drive home his idea, he felt it was necessary to show Blanco actually trying, if not to reform at least to convince, his companions of the genuineness of his temporary conversion.

No one will deny that to the worst of "bad men" there come experiences of this sort, but they are rarely external in their manifestation. It is not the place of the present volume to criticise the ideas of dramatists, except in so far as they influence the form of the drama. Still, it may be asked, is this play convincing? It is not intended as a comedy, although it is amusing, nor is it primarily a character study: it is a sermon in play form.

GRANVILLE BARKER

H. Granville Barker was born at London in 1877. At an early age he became an actor in a provincial company. He first appeared on the London stage in 1892. Playing under Lewis Waller and Ben Greet, then with the Elizabethan Stage Society, and finally with Mrs. Campbell, he slowly rose in the theatrical world. During many years he produced plays and acted for the Stage Society, where he mounted many of Shaw's plays for the first time. In 1904, together with J. E. Vedrenne, he managed the Court Theater, where he made known to theater-goers many new plays by Shaw, Hankin, Barrie, Galsworthy, and himself. He has continued his managerial activities at the Duke of York's Theater, the Savoy—where he has succeeded signally in some Shaksperian revivals—the St. James's, and the Kingsway.

Granville Barker is a keen observer of life, possessing a remarkable talent for putting his ideas into dramatic shape. His best plays are faithful pictures of character: "The Voysey Inheritance" is one of the best portrayals of middle-class English family life of modern times; "Waste" is a tragedy with an essentially timely and interesting theme; "The Madras House" is an acute and penetrating comedy of character. Barker is not a devotee of the well-made play, for he carefully avoids the well-trodden

90

paths of Pinero; in certain plays, "The Madras House" especially, his work at first view appears amorphous and ineffective. Yet this comedy, formless in the conventional sense as it undoubtedly is, could not have been forced into the mould of such a play as "The Thunderbolt." In "Prunella" and "The Harlequinade," both collaborations, and in "At the Mitre," Barker has essayed the poetic drama with remarkable success.

PLAYS

THE WEATHER HEN (in collaboration with Berte Thomas, 1899).

Performed at the Manhattan Theater, New York 1900.

THE MARRYING OF ANN LEETE (1902).

PRUNELLA (in collaboration with Laurence Housman, 1904).

Performed at the Little Theater, New York 1913.

THE VOYSEY INHERITANCE (1905).

WASTE (1909).

THE MADRAS HOUSE (1910).

ROCOCO (1911).

Besides the above, Barker has adapted Schnitzler's "Anatol" (Kennerley) and, in collaboration with W. C. E. Wheeler, the same author's "Das Märchen." (Not published.) He has also written a dialogue, "At the Mitre," which was produced at the Fine Arts Theater, Chicago 1913. (Not published.)

"The Marrying of Ann Leete," "The Voysey Inheritance," and "Waste" are published by Kennerley as "Three Plays by Granville Barker"; "Prunella" is published by Duffield; "The Madras House" by Kennerley. "The Weather Hen" and "Rococo" and "The Harlequinade" are not published. "The Madras House" is included in "Chief Contemporary Dramatists" (Houghton Mifflin).

REFERENCES: Ashley Dukes, "Modern Dramatists" (Sergel); Archibald Henderson, "European Dramatists" (Stewart and Kidd); John Palmer," The Future of the Theater" (Bell, London); Ludwig Lewisohn, "The Modern Drama" (Huebsch); William Archer, "Playmaking" (Small, Maynard); P. P. Howe, "The Repertory Theater," and "Dramatic Portraits" (Kennerly); William Archer and Granville Barker, "Schemes and Estimates for a National Theater" (Duffield); Frank Wadleigh Chandler, "Aspects of Modern Drama" (Macmillan); Mario Borsa, "The English Stage of To-day" (Lane); Desmond McCarthy, "The Court Theater" (A. H. Bullen); Granville Barker, Introductions to "Three Plays of Maeterlinck" (Gowans and Grey), and his own editions of "A Midsummer Night's Dream," "Twelfth Night," and "A Winter's Tale" (Sidgwick and Jackson).—*Magazines: Bookman* (London), July, 1914; *Forum,* vol. xliv (p. 159); *Bookman* (New York), vol. xxxv (p. 195); *Fortnightly,* vol. xcv (p. 60) and vol. c (p. 100); *Nation,* vol. xci (p. 19), vol. xciv (p. 445); *Harper's Weekly,* vol. lvi (p. 6): *North American,* vol. cxcv (p. 5720); *Drama,* No. 2.

THE VOYSEY INHERITANCE

A play in five acts. First performed in 1905.

This young dramatist's work is undoubtedly among
the ablest achievements in the realm of recent British
drama; its freshness, its cleverness, its deft handling
of middle-class types, its theme, strike a new note in
drama. Unlike the didactic plays of Shaw, unlike the
fantasies of Barrie, or the rigid pieces of Galsworthy, " The Voysey Inheritance " is pure character
writing, literature in the true dramatic sense. It has
been only moderately successful, but this is due
largely to the fact that the audiences were behind
the dramatist: the play is European, in the larger
sense of the term.

1. In the Shaw outlines (pp. 72-4) some attention was given to the matter of stage-directions. In the English theater of to-day there are
three dramatists who use this method of affording
their readers a greater insight into the characters
than could be afforded in actual stage presentation:
Shaw, Barrie, and Granville Barker. Shaw refused
to rely upon the actors; Barrie, who has until recently refused to allow his plays to be printed,
felt that without the actors the reader could not
possibly re-create the necessary atmosphere;

Barker probably felt that owing to the failure
(from a practical viewpoint) of most of his plays,
it was his right to reconstruct the *milieu* by means
of words.

Such directions as the following must be very
annoying to the average manager:

> . . . *Relieved of his coat, Mr. Voysey carries to
> his table the bunch of beautiful roses he is accustomed
> to bring to the office three times a week, and places
> them for a moment only, near the bowl of water there
> ready to receive them, while he takes up his letters.*

A play intended only for the manager would, of
course, have no reference to the fact that Voysey
" *is accustomed to bring* " the flowers " *to the
office three times a week,*" as this cannot be *shown*
on the stage. Such directions are obviously for
the reader, or for such managers as are willing to
study the manuscript and endeavor to reproduce
the atmosphere which the dramatist has striven to
create.

The printed play often resembles the novel
or story in its narrative directions. Turn to the
opening of the second act of this play. Speaking
of the dining-room at Chislehurst, the author says:
" *It has the usual red-papered walls (like a reflection, they are, of the underdone beef so much con-
sumed within them*)," etc. While this is distinctly
outside the province of what can be done by the

stage carpenter, it should be advantageous to an
imaginative director.

Compare the stage directions of "Man and
Superman," "The Voysey Inheritance," and "The
Twelve-pound Look."

2. This play is a character-comedy, a play of
ideas, and a conversation piece. There are long
scenes which, strictly speaking, have little or
nothing to do with the play itself, but are they
necessarily superfluous? What has been the
dramatist's purpose?

Has the same author's "Waste" any superfluous scenes?

3. One of the signs and results of the "com-
mercialization" of the present-day English and
American stages is the reduction of the number of
characters in a play. Each character means another actor, and another twenty-five to five hundred dollars a week increase in the pay-roll. This
is of course not invariably the reason for the
existence of small casts in many modern plays:
often the dramatist needs but three, four, five, or
six characters, and takes pride in the fact that he
can construct a full-length piece without having
recourse to the rather facile Shaksperian method
of bringing in a character every time he thinks
he needs one. Jules Lemaître in "The Pardon,"
Hubert Henry Davies in "The Mollusc," and H.
S. Sheldon in "The Havoc," have written skilful

and artistic plays with—in the case of the first—
three, and in the latter, four characters only.
However, a manager will try his best to cut down
the cast as much as possible.

Can this be done to " The Voysey Inheritance "?
Take the character you consider the least impor-
tant from the play. How would the play suffer?
Take two, then three.

Do you think that Barker required all the characters he put into this play? If so, in what way?
That is, did he prefer to paint a picture of life,
regardless of the artistic arrangement of its com-
ponent elements, or did he imagine that the more
characters he introduced the more interesting
would the play be? Briefly, did he adopt the
dramatist's viewpoint, or the novelist's?

STEPHEN PHILLIPS

Stephen Phillips was born at Somertown, England, in 1867. After receiving his primary education at Peterborough, he joined F. R. Benson's company, in which he acted for some years. For a while he adopted the profession of army tutor, then devoted himself entirely to the writing of plays and poetry. At present he is editor of the *Poetry Review*.

Phillips is a phenomenon in the English theater of to-day: a poet who has partially succeeded on the stage. In a day when the theater public will not listen to poetry, he has dared to be poetic, but he has likewise had the good sense to mix with his poetry a generous infusion of truly dramatic qualities. In the words of E. E. Hale, Jr., he "may succeed on the stage, but it will be in spite of his poetry and not by reason of it."

PLAYS

PAOLO AND FRANCESCA (1899).
  Performed at the New Amsterdam Theater, New York 1906.
HEROD (1900).
  Performed at the Lyric Theater, New York 1909.
ULYSSES (1902).
  Performed at the Garden Theater, New York 1902.

THE SIN OF DAVID (1904).

NERO (1906).

FAUST (in collaboration with J. Comyns Carr, 1908).

PIETRO OF SIENA (1909).

THE KING (1910).

NERO'S MOTHER (1913).

THE ADVERSARY (1913).

HAROLD (1915).

Besides the above are: "The Last Heir," "The Bride of Lammermoor," "No. 6," and "Armageddon." The first of these has not been published, while the other two have not yet been produced. All the published plays are issued by Lane.

REFERENCES: E. E. Hale, Jr., "Dramatists of To-day" (Holt); William Archer, "Real Conversations" (Heinemann, London); Arthur Symons, "Studies in Prose and Verse" (Dutton); Clayton Hamilton, "The Theory of the Theater" (Holt); Brander Matthews, "The Historical Novel" (Scribner's); F. W. Chandler, "Aspects of Modern Drama" (Macmillan); Ludwig Lewisohn, "The Modern Drama" (Heubsch).—*Magazines: Atlantic,* vol. xcii (p. 120) and vol. cii (p. 809); *Fortnightly,* vol. xci (p. 337); *Arena,* vol. xxxiii (p. 474); *North American,* vol. clxxii (p. 794); *Bookman,* vol. xiii (p. 24); *Quarterly Review,* vol. cxcv (p. 486); *Poet-Lore,* vol. xii (p. 126); *Nation,* vol. lxx (p. 361); *Westminster,* vol. clvi (p. 187).

PAOLO AND FRANCESCA

A tragedy in four acts. First performed in 1902.

.It is a remarkable fact that although, since the very
beginnings of drama, plays have been written in
verse, the legitimacy of the " poetic drama " is still
called into question. There is, however, some ground
for such a discussion, yet it is undeniable that if a
play be good drama and good poetry it is " legitimate." Perhaps because of the naturalistic tendency
of the past twenty-five or thirty years, during which
the English poetic drama has been at its lowest ebb,
more " closet drama " than acting pieces have been
written than would otherwise have been the case,
merely because the form had fallen into disfavor with
theater-goers. When the great Victorian poets—
Tennyson, Browning, Swinburne, and Matthew
Arnold—wrote plays, they had only the vaguest notion of the exigencies of the stage: " Queen Mary,"
" A Blot in the 'Scutcheon," " Atalanta in Calydon,"
and " Empedocles " are written to appeal rather to
the ear and the intellect than to the eye and the more
elemental emotions. These poets were either unaware
that the dramatic form was totally different from the
lyric or epic, or they did not care to write plays
for the stage, preferring the " dramatic poem." For
the most part they failed to distinguish dramatic
dialogue from lyric and epic verse. Browning's lines

in " A Blot in the 'Scutcheon " reveal character, but
they fail to indicate " spiritual action." The resultant play gives one the impression of reading a
number of the poet's " Dramatic Monologues," strung
together upon a thread of story: in other words, he
gains nothing through casting his thoughts in what
appears to be play form.

Shakspere affords us the finest example of dramatic
dialogue: in the lines he reveals character, creates
atmosphere, indicates spiritual action, and advances
the story. The following random quotation from
" Macbeth " will serve as illustration of the point:

. . . The raven himself is hoarse
That croaks the fatal entrance of Duncan
Under my battlements. Come, you spirits
That tend on mortal thoughts, unsex me here,
And fill me, from the crown to the toe, top-full
Of direst cruelty! make thick my blood,
Stop up the access and passage to remorse,
That no compunctious visitings of nature
Shake my fell purpose, nor keep peace between
The effect and it! Come to my woman's breasts,
And take my milk for gall, you murdering ministers,
Wherever in your sightless substances
You wait on nature's mischief! Come, thick night,
And pall thee in the dunnest smoke of hell,
That my keen knife see not the wound it makes,
Nor heaven peep through the blanket of the dark,
To cry, " Hold, hold! "

Enter Macbeth.

Great Glamis! worthy Cawdor!

Greater than both, by the all-hail hereafter!
Thy letters have transported me beyond
This ignorant present, and I feel now
The future in the instant.

Stephen Phillips, in "Ulysses," "Herod," and
"Paolo and Francesca," has shown some gift for
dramatic dialogue; and as a dramatist, many particular scenes from these plays give evidence of a sense
of the theater and considerable skill in developing a
plot. Still "Paolo and Francesca," in many ways
this poet's finest effort, is far from a good play—in any
sense of the term—chiefly because Phillips the poet
stands out above Phillips the dramatist.

1. Most poetic plays are modeled, with certain
modifications, upon the plays of ancient Greece
or those of the age of Elizabeth, and Stephen
Phillips, being an Englishman, follows—even in
"Ulysses"—Elizabethan models.

As the story of Paolo and Francesca is well
known—it appears in Dante's "Divine Comedy"
—we are prepared for such mystic forebodings
(technically speaking, "preparation") as occupy
the greater part of the brief first act. First,
Paolo's desire to leave, his brother's anxiety, then
the scene (pp. 22-6) with Lucrezia, and that immediately following, with the blind Angela. There
is no need to leave the audience in doubt as to what
the story is to be: Angela's words supply the
necessary warning:

His face was dim: a twilight struggles back.
I see two lying dead upon a bier—
Slain suddenly, and in each other's arms. . . .
.   .   . He shall be
Not far to seek: yet perilous to find.
Unwillingly he comes a wooing: she
Unwillingly is wooed: yet shall they woo.
His kiss was on her lips ere she was born.

And Stephen Phillips, the dramatist, adds the stage-direction: " *Francesca, in passing, pauses and offers trinket to Angela, who shudders, letting it fall. Exeunt all but Angela, who remains staring before her.*" If there was the least shadow of doubt in the mind of the audience as to the truth of Angela's words, her action would dispel it.

2. So far, the story is compact and moving. The second act is well developed up to the second scene (p. 51), which takes up the plot as it was left in the first act. Giovanni is made aware of the identity of Francesca's fated lover. Then the scene changes—Shakspere's method again—to a more or less " comic relief " scene, written in prose. This interlude is followed by Paolo's soliloquy (pp. 59-61).

The soliloquy in modern plays is considered to be a confession of weakness on the part of the dramatist. It had hitherto been used largely as a makeshift by the dramatist who was unwilling or unable to reveal character or advance his plot by other and more natural means. Yet in the poetic drama it is permissible—that is, if it reveals character, creates atmosphere, or advances the story. Obviously, Paolo's speech reveals some character, but as a dramatic expedient its insertion at this critical point must be considered a blemish on the play. The point for the dramatist was, how to get Paolo to return to Francesca? The struggle goes on in Paolo's mind, and the poet has only to give words to the lover's thoughts and emotions. But in a play that is not sufficient. Just how this end was to be accomplished is not our business or intention to determine; yet the fact remains that a monologue is not sufficiently convincing, especially as the monologue leaves us in doubt as to the character's immediate intentions. Here is the end of the speech:

I cannot go; thrilling from Rimini,
A tender voice makes all the trumpets mute.
I cannot go from her: may not return.
O God! what is thy will upon me? Ah!
One path there is, a straight path to the dark.
There, in the ground, I can betray no more,
And there forever am I pure and cold.
The means! No dagger blow, nor violence shown
Upon my body to distress her eyes.
Under some potion gently will I die;
And they that find me dead shall lay me down
Beautiful as a sleeper at her feet.

3. The break in the middle of Act II was justifiable because of the contrast it afforded. The third act, however, should intensify the plot, draw the attention to the central idea, not because of a certain law of dramatic technic, but because the human mind demands this sort of synthesis. To start a story, develop it a little, then stop it, then play *around* it, is not only bad art but bad psychology: we demand a logical continuation of the story when it is once started. In place of this we have another contrast scene, which opens the act, then Giovanni's entrance (p. 70), and his rather unconvincing errand; the coincidence of his overhearing Paolo, then Paolo's soliloquy (p. 78), and finally Giovanni's scene with the messenger (pp. 80-1). This is all very ragged. Then—Scene 3 —there is a good dramatic scene. Note the " atmosphere " lines:

Francesca.—I cannot sleep, Nita; I will read here. Is it dawn yet? (*Nita sets lamp down.*)
Nita.—   No, lady: yet I see A flushing in the east.
Francesca.—   How still it is!
Nita.—This is the stillest time of night or day!

Toward the end of the act, the poet's mistake in crowding too many incidents into a small space becomes only too apparent; not only does the crowding confuse, but it occupies space which should be given, we feel, to the love scene. We are told, it is true, that the two " have to each other moved all night," but how much more telling and convincing would have been a longer scene between the lovers, such as D'Annunzio gave in his " Francesca da Rimini "!

4. That admirable love scene which should have supported the third act is placed instead in the otherwise admirable fourth.

5. There are lyrical passages throughout, not many it is true, which do not contribute to the story. Can you pick these out? On the other hand, there are dramatic lines and passages which are peculiarly apt and effective. Among these latter are:

Henceforward let no woman have two sons, (p. 51)

So still it is that we might almost hear
The sigh of all the sleepers in the world. (p. 85)

. . . You then that huddle all together
Like cattle against thunder—what hath chanced?
                              (p. 92)

Paolo.—Why did you shiver and turn sudden cold?
Francesca.—I felt a wind pass over me. (p. 111)

I did not know the dead could have such hair.
Hide them.   They look like children fast asleep.
                                        (p. 120)

These are lines that could not be so effective
were they not spoken by the right person under the
right circumstances.   Find further examples.

ST. JOHN HANKIN

St. John Emile Clavering Hankin was born in 1860 at Southampton. His early education was received in his native city, but he later attended Malvern College, and then Merton College at Oxford. After his graduation in 1890, he went to London, and entered the field of journalism. Four years later, he went to Calcutta, there pursuing his journalistic career. The following year he returned and began writing for *The Times* and *Punch*. In 1909, as a result of his neurasthenic condition, and in a fit of depression, he drowned himself.

Hankin is among the number of recent English dramatists whose aim it was to give to the stage plays of charm and individuality and containing a valuable comment on life. He allied himself with the pioneers of the Court Theater and the Stage Society, where innovations and attempts to break loose from the conventionalities of the day were freely accepted. Probably because of his premature death in 1909, Hankin has been a little too highly praised. John Drinkwater (in his introduction to the " Dramatic Works ") says: " St. John Hankin lived and wrote at the beginning of a new movement, and his permanent distinction in drama will be rather that of right endeavor and the recapture of just instincts than of full-bodied achievement . . . that he was one of the few who

first sought to bring back sincerity and a fit dignity
of form to the great art is a distinction of which he
will not easily be deprived." Hankin was more a
symptom than a finished product; yet his efforts to
produce life in an artistic and pleasing framework,
and his quaint wit, entitle him to a place among the
less important members of the advance guard.

PLAYS

THE TWO MR. WETHERBYS (1903).
  Performed at the Madison Square Theater, New
    York 1904.
THE RETURN OF THE PRODIGAL (1905).
THE CHARITY THAT BEGAN AT HOME (1906).
THE CASSILIS ENGAGEMENT (1907).
THE CONSTANT LOVER (1912).
THE LAST OF THE DE MULLINS (1908).
THE BURGLAR WHO FAILED (1908).
THOMPSON (finished by George Calderon).
  Not performed.
  The definitive edition of the " Dramatic Works of
St. John Hankin, with an Introduction by John
Drinkwater " is published in three volumes by Kenner-
ley. " Thompson " is published separately by the
same publisher. Samuel French publishes cheap
paper editions of " The Return of the Prodigal," " The
Cassilis Engagement," " The Charity That Began at
Home," and " The Two Mr. Wetherbys."
  REFERENCES: Introduction to the " Dramatic
Works "; P. P. Howe, " Dramatic Portraits," " The

Repertory Theater" (Kennerley); J. M. Kennedy, "English Literature, 1880-1905" (Stephen Swift, London); Charlton Andrews, "The Drama To-day" (Lippincott); Mario Borsa, "The English Stage of To-day" (Lane); Desmond McCarthy, "The Court Theater" (Sidgwick and Jackson, London); Archibald Henderson, "The Changing Drama" (Holt).— *Magazines: Fortnightly,* vol. lxxxvi (p. 1055), vol. xc (p. 1038); *Living Age,* vol. cclxii (p. 36), vol. cclxxx (p. 781); *Nation,* vol. xcvi (p. 315); *North American,* vol. cxcvii (p. 78); *Forum,* vol. xlviii (p. 713).

THE CASSILIS ENGAGEMENT

A comedy in four acts. First performed in 1907.

The influence of Oscar Wilde is evident. Lady
Remenham's "Engagements are such troublesome
things. They sometimes even lead to marriage. But
we'll hope it won't be as bad as that in this case," is
decidedly reminiscent. The characters are mostly
types; still, in most of Hankin's plays there is an
effort to break away from the mere lay-figures of
Wilde and infuse into them the breath of life. The
prodigal in "The Return of the Prodigal," Ethel
and Mrs. Cassilis in the comedy under discussion, are
human beings, even if Lady Remenham, Mrs. Bor-
ridge, and Geoffrey are time-worn types.

1. Hankin has theorized on the writing of plays,
and his words possess added interest and value in
connection with the study of "The Cassilis Engagement." He once said: "I select an episode
in the life of one of my characters or a group of
characters, when something of importance to their
future has to be decided, and I ring up my curtain. Having shown how it was decided, and why
it was so decided, I ring it down again." This
comedy is clear and unified—quite in accordance
with the dramatist's theory—but it will be well to

inquire into the exact methods whereby he attained the desired end.

What is the " episode " round which this play was built? Where is it first referred to—that is, where is the theme announced? Is it made clear through a " raisonneur," or is it evolved in action or in apparently casual conversation? Are we asked to interest ourselves in a " character," or a " group of characters " ? Which character, and which group of characters?

Could the author have advantageously begun his play at an earlier or later time than he did? That is, was his curtain " rung up " at the most interesting and opportune moment of the episode?

How was the " something of importance to their future " decided? By what means has the dramatist worked out his stated central idea?

2. The " curtains " in this play deserve especial attention: a crisp and pregnant phrase, an incident, a mysterious word—each causes the audience to await impatiently the opening of the next act. Notice with what care, apparently artless, the first act is terminated. Mrs. Cassilis's " Marry her!—Nonsense, my dear Margaret," instantly attracts our attention and directs our interest to the speaker. We wish to know precisely how Geoffrey and Ethel are to be " cured," and want to see how the (evidently) clever Mrs. Cassilis is

to effect the cure. Plot interest, as distinguished
from character interest, is here introduced.

In what way is the second act remarkable? The
third?

It is as important to close a play without arousing further interest as to close each of the preceding acts in the reverse manner. There should
be an air of finality which precludes further curiosity; we should have no definite wish to inquire
into the future. To lead an audience to expect
more, after the play is over, is as fatal as to
deprive it of sufficient curiosity after the first act.
The dramatist must know where to end his play.
In a tragedy this particular point is not difficult
to determine, for a tragedy usually ends in the
death or failure of the protagonist. For centuries
comedies have ended with the union of lover and
sweetheart, who had, during one, two, three, four,
or five acts, been kept apart more or less skilfully
by the hand of the dramatist. Of recent years,
writers, even of comedy, have begun to discard
the conventional notion that the united lovers married and lived happy ever after, and have sought
a closer approximation to life. They have come
to realize that, as Emile Faguet once remarked,
the marriage is not the end but the beginning of
trouble. To mention two random instances,
Maurice Donnay's "Lovers" ("Amants") and
Henry Bataille's "Poliche" end with a scene where

the lovers separate; they do this because only by an amicable breaking-off can they be assured of true and lasting happiness. Here the dramatists have repudiated marriage as the balm for wounded hearts.

Hankin disliked " happy endings." (See his article on this subject in the third volume of the " Dramatic Works.") Is the ending of " The Cassilis Engagement " satisfactory, psychologically and artistically?

3. Analyze the third act, and determine, so far as possible, the following questions: How much of the story is carried on in pantomime through the stage-directions? Could, for example, the " Bye-play for Ethel's song," etc. (p. 78, French's edition, p. 193, Vol. II, " Dramatic Works ") have been worked out in dialogue? Is the dumb-show more effective than ordinary dialogue would be? Is Ethel's change of attitude likely and convincing?

Compare " The Cassilis Engagement " as a study in character and technic with the same author's " The Return of the Prodigal."

C. HADDON CHAMBERS

Charles Haddon Chambers was born at Stanmore, New South Wales, in 1860. He was educated privately and at Sydney. In 1875 he entered the Civil Service. Five years later he visited England. In 1882 he definitely settled there and became a journalist, writer of stories, and dramatist.

Chambers is one of the popular playwrights who have added little to the theater save a number of amusing and sentimental comedies. His technic differs little from that of Pinero, except that it is not so highly developed. Besides writing three or four plays of some value as contemporary pictures of manners, he has adapted a number of French plays, taking from them the flavor of the original and substituting a British atmosphere in order to render them acceptable to a public, in America as well as in England, which is not as yet ready to judge works of art according to European standards.

PLAYS

ONE OF THEM (1886).

THE OPEN GATE (1887).

> Performed at the Broadway Theater, New York 1890.

CAPTAIN SWIFT (1888).

> Performed at the Madison Square Theater, New York 1888.

THE IDLER (1890).

> Performed at the Lyceum Theater, New York 1890.

THE HONOURABLE HERBERT (1891).

THE OLD LADY (1892).

THE PIPE OF PEACE (1892).

Performed at the Lyceum Theater, New York 1892.

JOHN-A-DREAMS (1894).

Performed at the Empire Theater, New York 1895.

THE TYRANNY OF TEARS (1899).

Performed at the Empire Theater, New York 1899.

THE AWAKENING (1901).

THE GOLDEN SILENCE (1903).

SIR ANTHONY (1906).

PASSERS-BY (1911).

Performed at the Criterion Theater, New York 1911.

Collaborated in the following:

DEVIL CARESFOOT (1887).

THE QUEEN OF MANOA (1892).

THE FATAL CARD (1894).

Performed at the Academy of Music, New York 1895.

BOYS TOGETHER (1896).

THE DAYS OF THE DUKE (1897).

Chambers has adapted a number of French plays and dramatized a few novels.

"The Idler," "Captain Swift," "The Open Gate," and "Sir Anthony," are published by Samuel French; "The Tyranny of Tears" and "The Awakening" by Walter H. Baker; "Passers-By" by Brentano's.

REFERENCE: Introduction to the Baker edition of "The Tyranny of Tears."—*Magazines: Bookman,* vol. xxxiv (p. 242), vol. xxxviii (p. 264); *McClure's,* vol. xlii (p. 51).

THE TYRANNY OF TEARS

The play is technically of the Pinero-Jones school; still, it has a freshness which is sometimes lacking in cleverer and more brilliant plays. There are no surprises, there is little to astound or arouse to deep reflection. Based upon one of those inherent human qualities easily recognized by an average audience, it pursues its agreeable way through four pleasing acts.

1. In dealing with a conventional comedy of this sort it is fitting that conventional standards be applied to it. It will be seen that such plays as Elizabeth Baker's " Chains " and certain pieces of Granville Barker cannot so easily be measured according to older standards, but practically all the works of Jones, Pinero, Chambers, Davies, and Somerset Maugham, are easy to classify. Nor need this imply any detraction from their merits; originality in itself is little enough. While there is nothing new under the sun there may be new angles of vision, but a dramatist who chooses to view life from his new-found angle may be able to lay no better claim upon our admiration than that he has discovered a new *manner*. It is infinitely better to write a good play founded upon old and accepted formulas than a poor play

upon new and untried ones. The dramatist who writes conventional plays has the form ready at hand, and may proceed at once to attack the matter. A play by Pinero or Jones may almost invariably be counted upon to be masterly in form, and we may, as Bernard Shaw once said of the latter's plays, attack the matter without troubling about the manner.

" The Tyranny of Tears " is a conventional comedy of character and sentiment. Determine whether the dramatist has wished his audience to be more interested in the story, or the characters. What foundation is there for your opinion? Does Chambers intend to write a play showing how a man may be tyrannized over by a loving wife, or is he rather concerned with a story, into which he has allowed an idea, as it were, to wander?

2. Few more striking instances of the basic difference between French and English temperament and ideas can be found than by comparing the treatment of a similar theme in this play and in Porto-Riche's " Amoureuse." The Frenchman is concerned chiefly with the sexual side of the marriage, and insists that Etienne is forced to remain with his wife because she is still physically attractive to him. Chambers calls this attraction " tears " and makes of the story a pleasant and innocuous comedy. Porto-Riche goes straight to the heart of the question. In Anglo-

Saxon countries the problem would appear much
as Chambers has related it, while in Latin lands it
would more closely resemble Porto-Riche's treatment.   Chambers could not have written " Amoureuse " because he doubtless lacked the insight, and
would not have written it, even had the censor
passed it.   On the other hand, Porto-Riche would
not have wasted his time on what he would doubtless consider a prudish and trivial piece of work
like " The Tyranny of Tears."

3. In Professor Brander Matthews' " A Study
of the Drama," the author divides certain parts
of dialogue, after the manner of the French critics, into three kinds: *Mots de caractère*, *Mots de
situation*, and *Mots d'esprit*.   He says (p. 126):
" The French, among whom the critical faculty
is more acutely developed than among other peo-
ples, have a larger vocabulary of critical terms
than there is in any other language; and they
have devised a classification of certain of the effects of dialogue which are common to every type
of comic play.   They call a jest which evokes
laughter a *mot*, and they make a distinction which
is not easy to render in English between *mots
d'esprit*, *mots de situation*, and *mots de caractère*.
The *mot d'esprit* is the witticism pure and simple,
existing for its own sake, and detachable from its
context—like the remark of one of the characters
in ' Lady Windermere's Fan ': ' I can resist every-

thing—except temptation.' The *mot de situation*
is the phrase which is funny solely because it is
spoken at that particular moment in the setting
forth of the story, like the ' What the devil was
he doing in that galley? ' which is not laughter-
provoking in itself and apart from the incident
calling it forth, but which arouses peals of merri-
ment in its proper place in Molière's ' Scapin.'
And the *mot de caractère* is the phrase which
makes us laugh because it is the intense expression,
at the moment, of the individuality of the person
who speaks it—like the retort of the wife to her
sister in the ' Comedy of Errors,' when she has been
roundly abusing her husband.   Luciana satirically
comments that a man no better than this is no
great loss to be bewailed.   Whereupon Adriana,
smiling through her tears, returns: ' Ah, but I
think him better than I say—' a line which gets its
laugh, of course, but which lingers in the memory
as a sudden revelation of the underlying character
of the speaker.''

There are very few comic pieces which do not
contain many examples of these three sorts of *mot*,
and few other types of drama which fail to include
mots de situation.   These are necessary; while
mots de caractère are, though they may be interesting and amusing, and *mots d'esprit* laughter-
provoking, more or less in the nature of accessories.   The least necessary of all are the *mots*

d'esprit: it is a regrettable fact that Oscar Wilde occasionally marred scenes in his best comedies by introducing too many. The second act of " Lady Windermere's Fan," the first part of the third act of the same play, together with the first act of " A Woman of No Importance," are examples of this.

In the present play find examples of the three kinds of *mots* and determine which are the more necessary to the unity of the plot. Are there any superfluous *mots:* phrases, repartees, or epigrams which, if omitted, would in no manner mar the total effect?

4. Study the " curtains " throughout. Is the rise of the action, the tension in plot, increased, crisis by crisis, as it is in Sudermann's " Magda " and Pinero's " The Second Mrs. Tanqueray," or is it apparently disjointed and sudden as in Becque's " The Crows " and Wedekind's " The Awakening of Spring "?

HUBERT HENRY DAVIES

Hubert Henry Davies was born in 1869. He first entered the field of journalism, and pursued his profession in the United States for a number of years. Since 1899, when his first play, " A Dream of Love," was produced, until the present, he has enjoyed numerous successes.

Davies possesses a fastidious sense of form and literary style in his comparatively few comedies. He is not an innovator, he is content to accept the conventions as applied to comedies of manners as he finds them, and not venture abroad in quest of new methods or new ideas. He is always pleasantly conventional, although in his best plays—" The Mollusc," " Mrs. Gorringe's Necklace," " Doormats," and " Captain Drew on Leave "—there is ever some original treatment of character, some interesting underlying idea. " Doormats " sets forth the idea expressed by one of its personages: ". . . Some people have a genius for giving. Others a talent for taking. You can't not be whichever kind you are, any more than you can change your sex. You and I are amongst those who *must give.* . . . Doormats I always call them to myself." " Captain Drew on Leave " is more ambitious and conventional; it is the story of a good-hearted adventurer who falls in love with a married woman: he learns to value true affection, she to return to her husband, a stronger and nobler woman. Davies comes as something of a relief from the rather stiff, if broader, plays of Pinero, and from the occasionally tiresome efforts to evolve a new style of drama.

PLAYS

A DREAM OF LOVE (1899).

FIFTY YEARS AGO (1901).

COUSIN KATE (1903).

Performed, with Ethel Barrymore, at Daly's Theater, New York 1903.

MRS. GORRINGE'S NECKLACE (1903).

Performed at the Lyceum Theater, New York 1904.

CYNTHIA (1903).

Performed at the Madison Square Theater, New York 1903.

CAPTAIN DREW ON LEAVE (1905).

THE MOLLUSC (1907).

Performed at the Garrick Theater, New York 1908.

LADY EPPING'S LAWSUIT (1908).

BEVIS (1909).

A SINGLE MAN (1910).

Performed, with John Drew, at the Empire Theater, New York 1911.

DOORMATS (1912).

OUTCAST (1914).

Performed, with Elsie Ferguson, at the Lyceum Theater, New York 1914.

"Cousin Kate," " Mrs. Gorringe's Necklace," " Captain Drew on Leave," " The Mollusc," " Lady

Epping's Lawsuit," and " A Single Man " are published separately by Walter H. Baker, Boston.

REFERENCE: P. P. Howe, " Dramatic Portraits " (Kennerley).—*Magazines: North American,* vol. cci (p. 85); *New Republic,* vol. i (p. 23); *Bookman,* vol. xxxiv (p. 243).

THE MOLLUSC

A comedy in three acts. First performed in 1907.

As a technical feat there are few plays in the realm of recent English drama so neatly balanced, so economical, as " The Mollusc." It is unquestionably, by reason of its dramatic reticence, its charming style and its delicately handled theme, Davies's masterpiece.

1. The Aristotelian Unities—Time, Place, and Action—are here as closely adhered to as in Charles Rann Kennedy's " The Servant in the House," and a good deal more so than in Shaw's " Getting Married." True, the time of the last act is one week later, but this is really a minor detail. The Place is " Mrs. Baxter's sitting-room," the Action, Tom's " education of a mollusc." The first act shows us the mollusc, the second the struggle between Tom and the mollusc and Tom's temporary defeat, the third, his ultimate victory. Nothing could be clearer or more succinctly stated.

Compare the first act of this play with that of " The Second Mrs. Tanqueray." Could Pinero have learned anything about constructing a first act from Davies? What?

2. For the past twenty-five years or so, as has been said (p. 95), there is a tendency to lessen the number of characters in plays. The point has already been discussed, but it may be further remarked that a true artist loves his limitations: that Davies took pleasure in restricting himself to the use of but four personages, that Lemaître in " The Pardon " enjoyed the game of making only three carry the plot of a full-length play. This is vastly more difficult than it used to be. Many classical plays, from Æschylus to Sheridan, show a striking disregard for the time-scheme; Shakspere was often notoriously neglectful in this respect: a character might enter a room or a street from nowhere and go nowhere, and might return in an impossibly short time. While it is of course necessary to accept the convention of the foreshortening of time on the stage, we are unwilling—nowadays at least —to accept unmotivated and otherwise impossible entrances and exits. Now we require to know whence comes a character, how he happens to be where he is; if he leaves, his errand must be clear; if we are given to understand that he will return in half an hour, he must not come in two minutes later. (This, by the way, is the reason that on the stage very few clocks ever run.) In " The Mollusc," the comings and goings of each person are satisfactorily accounted for.

Work out the time-scheme of "Macbeth" or "Hamlet."

3. Closely allied with the subject of time is the general consideration of character-motivation. Why do people behave as they do? In life and on the stage? The difference between a conventional dramatist and one who has something novel to say, is that in the first instance his characters act according to set ideas, or according as they have acted in other plays. A good dramatist will inform us exactly why A behaved as he did under the circumstances; a psychologist, like François de Curel or Ibsen, will delve still deeper and reveal hidden corners of human character from the intuition which is genius, or from first-hand knowledge. Dramatists like Shakspere will merely draw a synthetic picture of life: the characters *are*, they behave as they do because they are what they are. In "Hamlet," the Prince reveals his thoughts and feelings in his speeches and his actions: he merely speaks his mind. If Hamlet were a conventional sort of man he would have killed his uncle; if "Hamlet" the play were a conventional play, the Prince would kill the murderer because the facts known to Hamlet would be sufficient to motivate the revenge. But Shakspere knew Hamlet's mind and revealed it to us through the character.

If we are made to feel that Zoe Blundell's suicide is natural—that is, if the events which led up to it allowed her to do nothing else, she being what she was—then " Mid-Channel " is well-motivated; if Cyrano's compliance with Roxane's request that he protect her lover is in accordance with Cyrano's character, then that act on his part is well motivated.

Study the motivation in " The Mollusc," in Shaw's " Man and Superman," and in Jones's " The Liars."

JOHN GALSWORTHY

John Galsworthy was born at Coombe, Surrey, in 1867. He received his education first at Harrow, then at Oxford, from which he was graduated in 1889. His first intention was to practise law, and in 1890 he was called to the bar. He says: " I read in various chambers, practised almost not at all, and disliked my profession thoroughly." Being in a position to do so, he began to travel, and visited a number of countries in all parts of the world. Some time later he began to turn his attention to writing, and in 1899 printed his first work, the novel " Jocelyn." This was followed by a short novel and a volume of short stories. Before the production of his first play he wrote four other novels; some of them—" The Country House " and " The Man of Property," for instance—must surely take rank among the finest literary achievements of the age. Since 1906, the date of " The Silver Box," Galsworthy has produced in turn collections of essays, stories, novels, plays, and poems.

Galsworthy is one of the sincerest and most straightforward of writers; literary, in the best sense of the word, clear, simple, and direct, he never fails to impress his readers and his audience with the meaning and importance of the play or novel under consideration. He is humanitarian in the broadest sense of the word: he is more than a socialist or a reformer, he is a sympathetic artist. In his plays he assumes so fair an attitude toward his characters and his audience that he at times almost fails to convince; in his dramatic style his reticence is occasionally so great that he incurs the danger of under-emphasis. Galsworthy is so sensitive that he perhaps over-estimates the sensitiveness of his audience. He is altogether one of the finest intellects and dramatic forces of the English stage.

PLAYS

THE SILVER BOX (1906).
> Performed, with Ethel Barrymore, at the Empire Theater, New York 1907.

JOY (1907).
> Performed by the University of Chicago Dramatic Club 1911.

STRIFE (1909).
> Performed at the New Theater, New York 1910.

JUSTICE (1910).
> Performed by the Hull House Players, Chicago 1911.

THE PIGEON (1912).
> Performed at the Little Theater, New York 1912.

THE ELDEST SON (1912).

THE FUGITIVE (1913).

THE MOB (1914).

A one-act play, " The Little Dream " (1911), completes the list.

" The Silver Box," " Joy," and " Strife " are published in a single volume by Putnam; " Justice," " The Little Dream," and " The Eldest Son " in " Plays,

Second Series " by Scribner's; " The Pigeon," " The
Fugitive," and " The Mob," in " Plays, Third Series "
by Scribner's. " Strife " is tncluded in " Chief Contemporary Dramatists " (Houghton Mifflin).

REFERENCES: Anonymous, " John Galsworthy, a
Sketch of His Life and His Works " (Scribner's);
Ashley Dukes, " Modern Dramatists " (Sergel); P. P.
Howe, " The Repertory Theater " (Kennerley) and
" Dramatic Portraits (Kennerley); Sheila Kaye-
Smith, " John Galsworthy " (Holt); John Palmer,
" The Future of the Theater " (Bell, London); Edwin
Björkman, " Is There Anything New Under the
Sun? " (Kennerley); Charlton Andrews, " The
Drama To-day " (Lippincott); William Archer,
" Playmaking " (Small, Maynard); Emma Goldman,
" The Social Significance of the Modern Drama "
(Badger); C. H. Herford, in " Essays and Studies
by Members of the English Association " (Oxford
University Press); Frank Wadleigh Chandler, " As-
pects of Modern Drama " (Macmillan); Clayton
Hamilton, " Studies in Stagecraft " (Holt); Archi-
bald Henderson, " The Changing Drama " (Holt);
Ludwig Lewisohn, " The Modern Drama " (Huebsch).
—*Magazines:* *Fortnightly,* vol. xci (p. 971), vol.
lxxxix (p. 627); *Current Literature,* vol. xlviii (p.
81); *Harper's Weekly,* vol. lvi (p. 6); *Outlook,* vol. c
(p. 608); *Literary Digest,* vol. xliv (p. 592); *Book
News Monthly,* vol. xxx (p. 771); *The World To-day,*
vol. xxi (p. 995); *Review of Reviews,* vol. lviii (p.
634); *Bookman,* vol. xxxv (p. 203); *Living Age,* vol.
cclxiv (p. 607); *Survey,* vol. xxiii (p. 705).

STRIFE

A drama in three acts. First performed in 1909.

In his essay, "Some Platitudes Concerning Drama" (in "The Inn of Tranquillity"), Galsworthy says: "A Drama must be shaped so as to have a spire of meaning. Every grouping of life and character has its inherent moral; and the business of the dramatist is so to pose the group as to bring that moral poignantly to the light of day. Such is the moral that exhales from plays like 'Lear,' 'Hamlet,' and 'Macbeth.'" As "Strife" is a peculiarly apt illustration of its author's theories as set forth in this essay, let us inquire into its structure, its development, and its moral.

1. "Strife" is an eminently fair and just arrangement of acts, facts, motives, and opinions, focusing up to "a spire of meaning," bearing upon the struggle between capital and labor. Galsworthy's first care was to set before his audience a clear statement, without taking sides with one party or the other. He mentions in the essay above quoted three courses which are open to the dramatist: (1) to give the public what it wants; (2) to give it what he thinks it ought to have, and (3) "to set before the public no cut-and-dried

codes, but the phenomena of life and character, selected and combined, *but not distorted*, by the dramatist's outlook, set down without fear, favor, or prejudice, leaving the public to draw such poor moral as nature may afford. This third method requires a certain detachment; it requires a sympathy with, a love of, and a curiosity as to, things for their own sake; it requires a far view, together with patient industry, for no immediately practical result."

2. That "certain detachment" is to be seen throughout "Strife." The dramatist's "sympathy with . . . things for their own sake" is observed in the balance of the scenes. For example, we are first made to see the representatives of capital, then Harness is introduced, and, a moment later, "the men." First the capitalists' side is heard, then the workingmen's. Within a few pages of the end of the act there is a deadlock between the contending parties; then Enid is brought in. Enid presents another aspect of the question; she, the daughter of Anthony, the head of the capitalists, may be termed the "human element." "We see *all* the distress," she says. "You remember my maid Annie, who married Roberts? It's so wretched, her heart's weak; since the strike began, she hasn't even been getting proper food." In the second act Enid is in the Roberts' cottage. Again the author's detachment is evident: he does not senti-

mentalize upon the workingmen, any more than he over-emphasizes the obduracy of the Board. If he feels that some human element is necessary, for the sake of truth and dramatic contrast, he allows the gentle and very human Enid (even the name is indicative of her character) to do the sentimentalizing. And again Galsworthy the practical dramatist follows the rules of Galsworthy the theorist: " The art of writing true dramatic dialogue is an austere art, denying itself all license, grudging every sentence devoted to the mere machinery of the play, suppressing all jokes and epigrams severed from character, relying for fun and pathos on the fun and tears of life. From start to finish good dialogue is hand-made, like good lace; clear, of fine texture, furthering with each thread the harmony and strength of a design to which all must be subordinated."

Throughout the first scene of the second act the characters of the people are laid bare with admirable clear-sightedness and detachment of vision. If the poor are in a bad condition, it is somewhat the fault of their pride and dogged tenacity. Madge Thomas's reply, " What suffering? . . . Who said there was suffering? " reveals a person much nearer to actual life than would that of a whining and humble woman.

In brief, then, Galsworthy shows that if the rich are hard, they have a modicum of the milk of human kindness, and that if the poor are miserable, they are at times stubborn and haughty.

3. Further on in the same essay the author remarks: " Now, true dramatic action is what characters do, at once contrary, as it were, to expectation and yet because they have already done other things." Galsworthy means here that the dramatist should not invent situations and adhere to a fixed plan when he is dealing with units which are intended to represent human beings. When, therefore, a character acts " contrary, as it were, to expectation," it is because we, the audience, do not know their true character. It is by means of unexpected turns and the revelation of motives hitherto unknown to the audience, that a dramatist paints character: he unrolls it, and the personages *develop*. Again this author's wide sympathy with life urges him to state that it is pretty difficult to determine just what a human being *will* do next.

Follow carefully the scenes in which Roberts, or any other of the principal characters, appears, bearing in mind the remarks above quoted.

4. In " Strife," what is the " spire of meaning "? What is the " inherent moral "? Was Galsworthy more interested in the moral than the characters? Or did he wish merely to exhibit a certain " grouping of life and characters "?

THE PIGEON

A fantasy in three acts. First performed in 1912.

In a little poem ("A Prayer") Galsworthy, the poet, asks that he may be given "to understand." All of Galsworthy's plays are evidently written by a man who wishes to dig beneath the surface, to learn to understand and help others to do so. Together with this view of life, the author's dramatic technic is intimately bound up. We have already seen how a dramatist should hold himself somewhat aloof from life in order to see it fairly: "Strife" is the best of this dramatist's plays to exemplify his attitude and his workmanship. "The Pigeon," "a fantasy in conception and a realistic play in execution," in Galsworthy's own words, is much less a cold expression of facts than "Strife." Its very theme is human charity. If one seeks some definite preachment of philanthropy—such as Brieux gave in "Les Bienfaiteurs"—the play will puzzle: the author shows only a "grouping of life and character," and allows us to seek out the "inherent moral." At the end, Wellwyn is as hopeless as he was at first, the flower-girl and her miserable companions are no nearer to a solution of the problem than before the curtain rose. Had Brieux or Hervieu written the play they would undoubtedly have offered some sort of moral, suggested some remedy; Galsworthy is content with affording us some insight into the thoughts and feelings of three hopeless waifs.

1. The first act is a work of art: Galsworthy never wrote a better act. The tag-end of a scene supposed to have passed just before the curtain rose, opens it; then Wellwyn and his daughter are briefly introduced in a page or two. There is no " exposition " in the conventional sense of the word: the characters evolve through the medium of dialogue that is " spiritual action." There is no superfluous word: each syllable counts. This is truly " austere art."

Take another passage from the author's theory: " The aim of the dramatist in employing it [naturalistic technic] is obviously to create such an illusion of actual life passing on the stage as to compel the spectator to pass through an experience of his own, to think, and talk, and move with the people he sees, thinking, talking, and moving in front of him. A false phrase, a single word out of tune or time, will destroy that illusion and spoil the surface as surely as a stone heaved into a still pond shatters the image seen there. . . . It is easy enough to *reproduce* the exact conversation and movements of persons in a room; it is desperately hard to *produce* the perfectly natural conversation and movements of those persons, when each natural phrase spoken and each natural movement made has not only to contribute toward the growth and perfection of a drama's soul, but also to be a revelation, phrase by phrase, movement by movement, of essential traits of character. To put it another way, naturalistic art, when alive, indeed to be alive at all, is simply the art of manipulating a procession of most delicate symbols."

2. If the writer of "Strife" and "The Pigeon" has succeeded—and he has—in abiding by his professed principles, it might be well to look into the validity of these principles. One final quotation: "We want no more bastard drama; no more attempts to dress out the simple dignity of everyday life in the peacock's feathers of false lyricism; no more straw-stuffed heroes or heroines; no more rabbits and goldfish from the conjurer's pockets, nor any limelight. Let us have starlight, moonlight, sunlight, and the light of our own self-respects." Galsworthy, in a word, is the enemy of all that is false in the theater of "theatricality." In his plays, there is ever a conscious effort to avoid effects, "big scenes," conventional dialogue and situations. Galsworthy seems afraid of a "curtain"; it has been aptly said of him that the "'curtains' seemed to hesitate to come down on anything that could possibly be mistaken for a climax." Yet it should be remembered that Galsworthy, disgusted with the falsity and triviality of a vast amount of present-day drama, was forced into his austere and reticent attitude. He has at

least shown that plays do not of necessity have to
be built according to time-worn formulas; he has
also proved that one of the surest methods of obtaining emphasis is—up to a certain point—to
under-emphasize. Mrs. Jones's " Oh! Sir!" which
closes " The Silver Box " is an admirable example.
If Galsworthy is an advocate of reticence he has
been forced partly by circumstances to be so.

In " The Pigeon " notice how the " curtains "
are managed. What elements of the usual " well-
made play " are observable in these? Compare
the second act of this play—as to its plot development—with the second act of " Candida."

3. In his book on " The Future of the Theater "
John Palmer states: " Their [the characters in
Galsworthy's plays] merit consists in all the com-
monplaces they do not utter, in all the obvious
things they do not do, in all the fine speeches
they do not make. In ' The Eldest Son ' Freda
says ' Oh, Bill!' and Bill makes the three following speeches: (1) ' Freda!'; (2) ' Good God!';
(3) ' By Jove! This is——' Whereupon the curtain saves him from committing his author any
further. These are tactics of masterly inactivity.
The scene is suggested by the players; and the
audience supplies the emotion. Mr. Galsworthy
has done nothing, except to suggest very clearly
that he has avoided doing anything wrong." The
last sentence here is an evident exaggeration, but

how much of the entire criticism applies to
" Strife " and " The Pigeon "? Has Galsworthy
in detaching himself, in his attempt to be scrupu-
lously exact and fair in his presentation of the
grouping of life he chose to exhibit, gone too far,
stood too far aloof, and lost that personal element,
that touch of humanity, without which no art can
exist?

4. The following letter to the writer touching
upon the play now under consideration, may
throw some light on the " fantastic " element:
". . . About those dates in ' The Pigeon.'
Christmas Eve because of Ferrand's remark: ' HE
is come, Monsieur!' and the general tenor of
Wellwyn's acceptance of every kind of outcast.
New Year's Day because of Ferrand's remark:
' 'Appy New Year!' which marks the disappear-
ance of casual charity in favor of Institutionalism,
of the era of outcasts in favor of the era of reformers. April 1st because of the joke at the end
on the Humblemen which symbolizes the fact, or
rather the essence, of the play, that, while Wellwyn (representing sympathy and understanding)
is being ' plucked ' all through the play, he comes
out and knows he does, on top at the end, as the
only possible helper of the unhelpable." The
author maliciously adds: " I hope this is sufficiently
obscure! "

JOHN MASEFIELD

John Masefield was born at Ledbury, England. At the age of fourteen he ran away from home and went to sea. For a number of years he wandered from land to land, spending part of the time in the United States. Returning to England, he devoted his time to the writing of poems, novels, stories, and a few plays. In 1912 he won the Edmond de Polignac prize for his "Everlasting Mercy." Since that time, he has enjoyed the success and popularity which has so long been denied him.

Masefield's principal contribution to modern literature are his vigorous and original narrative poems—"The Everlasting Mercy," "The Widow in the Bye-Street," and "Dauber"—in which his sense of the tragic and the beautiful find their expression. Something of this is observable in his shorter poems, and in his novels, especially "The Street of To-day" and "Multitude and Solitude," and in his play, "The Tragedy of Nan." "Nan" comes as near to true tragedy as any English play of recent years. It is a play of remarkable power and beauty as regards conception and style; it is the work of a true poet. The author's belief that tragedy should be a vision of the heart of life is borne out in "Nan" with pitiless cruelty. Masefield's originality precludes to a certain extent the question of influences, but it might be well to suggest that his friend Synge had something to do with his style, and to draw a parallel between the love-scene in the second act of "Nan" and that in the last act of "The Playboy of the Western World." Masefield's other plays, "Mrs. Harrison" and "The Campden Wonder," more or less in the style of "Nan," and his historical poems, "Philip the King" and "The Tragedy of Pompey the Great," have only a relative stage value, although they are full of striking lines, good scenes, and vigorous poetic passages.

PLAYS

THE CAMPDEN WONDER (1907).

THE TRAGEDY OF NAN (1908).

Performed by the Gaiety Theater Company in Boston 1911.

MRS. HARRISON (1909).

THE TRAGEDY OF POMPEY THE GREAT (1910).

PHILIP THE KING (1914).

There is besides an adaptation of "The Witch," unpublished, from the Norwegian of Wiers Jennssen, 1910.

REFERENCES: John Galsworthy, "The Inn of Tranquillity" (Scribner); C. E. Montague, "Dramatic Values" (Macmillan); John Masefield, Preface to (new edition of) "Nan."—*Magazines: Athenæum,* Nov. 13, 1909; *Dial,* Dec. 16, 1910; *Bookman,* vol. xxxiii (p. 584); *Current Literature,* vol. lii (p. 710),

vol. liii (p. 457); *Survey,* vol. xxxi (p. 707); *Inde-*
pendent, vol. lxxii (p. 1158), vol. lxxiii (p. 533);
Living Age, vol. cclxxiv (p. 778), vol. cclxxx (p. 410);
Atlantic, vol. cxi (p. 489); *North American,* vol. cxcviii
(p. 375); *Yale Review* vol. ii (p. 560).

THE TRAGEDY OF NAN

A play in three acts. First performed in 1908.

" Tragedy," says Masefield in a note prefixed to a late edition of this play, " at its best is a vision of the heart of life. The heart of life can only be laid bare in the agony and exaltation of dreadful acts. The vision of agony, or spiritual contest, pushed beyond the limits of dying personality, is exalting and cleansing. It is only by such vision that a multitude can be brought to the passionate knowledge of things exalting and eternal." " The Tragedy of Nan " is an attempt " towards the achieving of that power " which " helps the genius of a race to obtain it, though the obtaining may be fifty years after the strivers are dead."

1. The above quotation indicates a different conception of tragedy from the one usually set forth. The exalting and cleansing element is Greek ; the " passionate knowledge of things exalting and eternal " with the insistence on " dreadful acts " as a necessary premise to the laying bare of the heart of life is in a manner Masefield's own twist to a well-known theory. The story of " Œdipus " is a series of " dreadful acts," but the difference lies in Masefield's belief that the audi-

ence should *see* these acts. In "Hamlet" and "Macbeth" they are usually relegated to the background. Possibly this new idea is a concession to the lack of imagination of modern audiences, who have become too well accustomed to realistic plays? In any event, this poet insists upon showing us the horrible scene where Nan forces Jenny to eat the tainted mutton pie.

What is gained through this procedure? How far has the dramatist adhered to his principles in this play?

2. As art is a synthesizing of life, all that is unessential must be omitted in order that the typical, the characteristic, may be brought into emphatic relief. In a play, where the incidents are supposed to cover a space of many hours, many days, or many years, the incidents which the dramatist chooses must be condensed into something less than two hours: he cannot waste a word or a gesture. This necessitates an acceptance on the part of the audience of the convention of foreshortening: that is, incidents, psychological changes, development of character, occupy much less time on the stage than they would in life. An hour may be easily assumed to pass in ten minutes; in a moment a character reaches a decision which in life might take him days or months to reach; young men and women fall in love at first sight with little or no regard to verisimilitude.

Needless to say, there must be sufficient motivation
to account for these sudden changes, or the audience will refuse to enter into the dramatist's pact.
In Shakspere's " Richard III," the Queen, who is
accompanying her husband's bier to the church,
is met by Richard, her husband's known murderer,
is wooed in less than ten minutes—successfully
wooed. This is too great a strain upon the credu-
lity of the audience, in spite of the fact that the
play is obviously melodrama. In Ibsen's " Doll's
House," Nora's change of mind covers less than
a week, but Ibsen takes good care to support her
final act with credible motivation.

In " Nan " is Dick's change of heart sufficiently
motivated? Notice what reasons the dramatist
sets forth; that is his defense, as it were. Still, is
his change acceptable?

3. The last act in a play is usually the shortest.
The reason for this is that the climax, which is in
ninety-nine cases out of a hundred at the end of
the penultimate act, brings the play to its highest
pitch of interest and suspense, and there remains
little to be accomplished in the last. *Dénouement*
is not so interesting as a rule as development.
Many plays fail because of an uninteresting or
anti-climactic final act. It is the business of the
dramatist to hold over some absorbing revelation,
or some long-awaited turn of affairs, in order
that his audience may await with impatience the

last rise of the curtain. In W. C. De Mille's " The Woman," this has been very skilfully accomplished.

How has Masefield succeeded? His last act is the longest in the play. What does he do to make it interesting?

It is well to ask one's self, as the curtain is falling on the penultimate act of a play, whether there is much more worth waiting for?

STANLEY HOUGHTON

Stanley Houghton was born at Ashton-upon-Mersey, in 1881. In 1897 he entered his father's office in Manchester, where he worked until 1912, as a salesman. The success of the production of " Hindle Wakes " that year led him to forsake the security of business for the uncertainties of a dramatist's existence. In 1913 he went to Paris, fell ill, recovered, returned to London in June. On his return to Paris, on the way to Venice, he fell ill again. After an attack of influenza and appendicitis, in Italy, he was brought to Manchester, where, in December, he died.

At the time of his death Houghton was one of the most promising of the younger generation of British dramatists. While it is true that " Hindle Wakes " is his finest achievement, his other plays—" Independent Means " and " The Younger Generation " especially—are by no means negligible. Houghton was seeking for liberty of thought, rather than liberty of dramatic form, but he never distorted that form for the sake of the idea. He had a distinct sense of the theater, a remarkable gift for dialogue, and keen insight into human character.

PLAYS

THE DEAR DEPARTED (1908).
INDEPENDENT MEANS (1909).

THE MASTER OF THE HOUSE (1910).

THE YOUNGER GENERATION (1910).

Performed in New York 1913.

FANCY FREE (1911).

HINDLE WAKES (1912).

Performed in New York 1912, and on tour 1913.

PHIPPS (1912).

Performed at the Princess Theater, New York 1914.

THE PERFECT CURE (1913).

THE FIFTH COMMANDMENT (1913).

Performed at the Little Theater, Chicago 1913.

TRUST THE PEOPLE (1913).

Not published.

A number of short and slight plays, unpublished, were produced by amateurs. " Marriages in the Making" was never produced.

" Hindle Wakes " is published by Luce, Boston. Houghton's collected works, in three volumes, are published by Constable, London. " Independent Means " and " The Younger Generation " and " Five One-act Plays " are published by Samuel French.

REFERENCES: Introduction to the collected works; John Palmer, " The Future of the Theater " (Bell, London).—*Magazines: Bookman,* vol. xxxvi (p. 641); *Manchester Playgoer,* vol. ii, No. 1; *Manchester Quarterly,* vol. xxxiii (p. 213); *Living Age,* vol. cclxxx (p. 413); *McClure's,* vol. xl (p. 69).

HINDLE WAKES

A play in three acts. First performed in 1912.

"Hindle Wakes" is one of the few plays of conspicuous merit which have come from the younger group of British dramatists. This play is original by reason of its theme (the same, by the way, as that treated in St. John Ervine's "The Magnanimous Lover" and Galsworthy's "The Eldest Son"), its telling dialogue, and its construction. The characters are well drawn, lifelike, thoroughly human.

1. It is only by comparison with such plays as "Sweet Lavender" that one can appreciate the immense advance made in dialogue in this play. The early Pinero play was considerably influenced by the very stilted style of Robertson and H. J. Byron; still, it purported to be realistic in treatment. Read the first five pages of "Sweet Lavender," then the first five of "Hindle Wakes." Then read the first five of "The Second Mrs. Tanqueray," which is intended to be still closer to "real life," and then read five more of the Houghton play. Again, read a scene from "The Thunderbolt" (Pinero), one of the few frankly realistic pictures of English middle-class society which Pinero has attempted, and read another

149

scene from "Hindle Wakes." Pinero cannot escape from the shackles of his predecessors; Houghton came to the theater with a fresh outlook on life, and few ideas about the "literary" style of dialogue.

Bearing in mind Henry Arthur Jones's remarks (pp. 42-3) on literature and the stage, determine in what respects this play is literature.

2. "Hindle Wakes," besides being a "slice of life" and an interesting story, is a "thesis play." This does not mean that the author wrote it solely to exploit an idea, or that he was so interested in the moral that he neglected any means to make the play an interesting spectacle: the idea serves only to increase the interest. Up to the very last of the play (p. 97, Luce edition) the author's solution is not made clear. This was Ibsen's method in the "Doll's House," where, up to the middle of the last act, Nora's sudden resolution was not hinted at. It is likely that if these dramatists had been more interested in the propagandist side of their work they would doubtless have foreshadowed the end earlier in the play: their enthusiasm would have led them into argument and discussion far before the end. But both Ibsen and Houghton allowed their plays to develop naturally up to what in a conventional play would have been the beginning of the usual end, and then—by a sudden turn—changed the whole *dénouement*.

What indications are there that Houghton was less concerned than Ibsen with the idea, as distinct from the play as a dramatic entertainment? Does Houghton adopt a moral attitude? An immoral attitude?

3. What is the advantage of dividing the first act into three scenes? Is there any necessity for combining these three parts into one act? Why could the author not have made each of these into a separate act? Why did he not divide the second and third acts into scenes?

4. In any thesis play there is a danger that characters speak a good deal more logically and with much more penetration than they would in life: the dramatist puts his own arguments into their mouths, and consequently distorts them as characters. What would ordinarily be the logic of their actions he often makes them reason out in a way which would be out of the question in any other place. The logical explanation of Fanny's conduct occurs in the last scene of this play (pp. 97-104). Notice the following dialogue.

Alan.— . . . you'd damage my prospects, and all that sort of thing. You can see that, can't you?

Fanny.—Ay! I can see it now you point it out. I hadn't thought of it before.

Alan.—Then, that isn't why you refused me?

Fanny.—Sorry to disappoint you, but it's not.

Alan.—I didn't see what else it could be.

Fanny.—Don't kid yourself, my lad! It isn't because I'm afraid of spoiling *your* life that I'm refusing you, but because I'm afraid of spoiling *mine!* That didn't occur to you?

Alan.—It didn't.

Fanny.—You never thought that anybody else could be as selfish as yourself.

Alan.—I may be very conceited, but I don't see how you can hurt yourself by wedding me. You'd come in for plenty of brass, anyhow.

Fanny.—I don't know as money's much to go by when it comes to a job of this sort. It's more important to get the right chap.

Alan.—You like me well enough?

Fanny.—Suppose it didn't last? Weddings brought about this road have a knack of turning out badly. Would you ever forget it was your father bade you marry me? No fear! You'd bear me a grudge all my life for that.

And again,

Alan.—But you didn't ever really love me?

Fanny.—Love you? Good Heavens, of course not! Why on earth should I love you? You were just some one to have a bit of fun with. You were an amusement—a lark.

Alan (shocked).—Fanny! Is that all you cared for me?

Fanny.—How much more did you care for me?

Alan.—But it's not the same. I'm a man.

Fanny.—You're a man, and I was your little fancy.

Well, I'm a woman, and *you* were *my* little fancy. You wouldn't prevent a woman enjoying herself as well as a man, if she takes it into her head?

Alan.—But do you mean to say that you didn't care any more for me than a fellow cares for any girl he happens to pick up?

Fanny.—Yes. Are you shocked?

Alan.—It's a bit thick; it is really!

Fanny.—You're a beauty to talk!

Alan.—It sounds so jolly immoral. I never thought of a girl looking on a chap just like that! I made sure you wanted to marry me if you got the chance. . . .

Is the dramatist forcing his characters (Fanny especially) to give utterance to ideas which they would scarcely be able to formulate, merely in order that the theme may be clear?

How far has an author the right to do this?

GITHA SOWERBY

Katherine Githa Sowerby (Mrs. John Kendall), daughter of John Sowerby, the artist, was born in Newcastle in Northumberland. In this vicinity she spent the early years of her life. Her first literary ventures were short stories for magazines and a number of books for children. Her first play, " Rutherford and Son," was produced at the Court Theater, in 1912, and was followed by a curtain-raiser, " Before Breakfast."

Githa Sowerby's one important play is among the most powerful works of the younger generation. It is representative of that group of plays which treats of the relation of parents and children—like " The Voysey Inheritance," " Hindle Wakes," " The Younger Generation," and " Milestones." This first attempt * of a young author is the more remarkable

* In a·letter to the author (Sept. 22, 1914) she writes: "'Rutherford and Son' was originally produced at the Court Theater in London for four matinées. It was then put up for a run at the Little Theater and moved on to the Vaudeville. In December of the same year Mr. Ames produced it at the Little Theater, New York, and it has since been on at Stockholm and Munich. It has been translated into nearly all European languages and should have been produced in Paris, St. Petersburg, and various other foreign towns about this time, but the war prevented or postponed this. . . . My first efforts were short stories for magazines and a number of books for children, prin-

when it is learned that the writer had practically no experience or knowledge of dramatic technic, and entered the field of drama from that of fiction.

PLAYS

RUTHERFORD AND SON (1912).

Performed at the Little Theater, New York 1912.

BEFORE BREAKFAST (1912).

REFERENCE: Clayton Hamilton, " Studies in Stagecraft" (Holt).—*Magazine: Bookman,* vol. xxxvi (p. 642).

cipally in verse. . . . I don't know what made me think of writing a play. I had no experience of the stage and no knowledge of plays or players beyond what can be gained by seeing plays. But writing both prose and verse was difficult and irksome to me, so I began ' Rutherford and Son.' I wrote it over a period of two years in my spare time as an experiment, with no hope whatever of its being produced. I wrote two acts, thought it was no good, and threw it aside—then a friend happened to read it, and urged me to finish it, which I did. . . ."

RUTHERFORD AND SON

A play in three acts. First performed in 1912.

It is only of late years that the "family drama" has received full and adequate treatment in England. For many years Pinero and Jones and Wilde were content to limit themselves almost exclusively to the "drawing-room" play, which they brought to a point whence further development seemed impossible. The younger dramatists, Galsworthy, Barker, Miss Baker, Miss Sowerby, Stanley Houghton, and others, modeling perhaps upon the plays of Ibsen, and certainly striving for greater freedom in subject-matter, went to the middle and lower classes for their inspiration, and produced works which differ radically from the "Mrs. Tanquerays" and "Mrs. Danes" of the former generation. "Rutherford and Son" is one of the most striking examples of the new school. It is, perhaps, a little too extreme, possibly over-emphasized, but its dramatic power is incontestable.

1. The "pathetic fallacy" in drama is unusually common. It is an easy and very obvious dramatic expedient. First acts of tragedies or serious plays of any kind often contain forebodings of the coming crisis. Random examples of this are "Macbeth," "Riders to the Sea," and

" Brand." In each of these plays the weather outside serves as a striking background for the action.

In " Rutherford and Son " the stage-directions
and the dialogue make us aware of the season: " *On
this particular evening in December,*" etc. (p. 8),
and, in the course of the opening scene, such lines
as " I wonder what it's like here when the sun
shines ! " and " It doesn't look as if the summer
ever came here," go far to create an atmosphere
of gloom.

In this first act is the creation of atmosphere
and local color too obvious? How far may a
dramatist legitimately call in the aid of natural
phenomena, in order to help the action of his
play?

2. The struggle, the clash of character upon
character which is one of the essentials of drama,
is introduced in the first act in an unusual fashion.
As a rule, the struggle is " exposed," or talked
about, early in the first act, then, later in that act,
or in the second, the clash actually begins. As a
matter of fact, the struggle in " Rutherford and
Son " is so vividly laid before the audience in the
first few pages, and especially in the scene between
Mary and young Rutherford, that it may be said
actually to have begun before the entrance of old
John Rutherford. So domineering and strong is
the old man's will, so plain are the results of its
exercise, that it stands before us, needing for

the time being, no further illustration. Then Richard enters (p. 25):

Ann.—. . . If he hadn't gone to the bank how would Rutherfords' ha' gone on?

John.—. . . Why should it go on?

Ann (*sharply*).—What's that?

John.—Why didn't he sell the place when he could have made a decent profit?

Ann (*scandalized*).—Sell Rutherfords'? Just let your father hear you.

John.—I don't care if he does. I never can imagine why he hangs on—working his soul out year after year.

Ann (*conclusively*).—It's his duty. . . .

John.—Duty—rot! He likes it. He's gone on too long. He couldn't stop and rest if he tried. When I make a few thousands out of this little idea of mine I'm going to have everything I want, and forget all about the dirt and the ugliness, the clatter and bang of the machinery, the sickening hot smell of the furnaces—all the things I've hated from my soul.

Already, and before old John Rutherford appears, the struggle has begun.

Compare the beginning of this parents-and-children struggle with that in Sudermann's "Magda" and Granville Barker's "The Voysey Inheritance."

3. A strike in the background serves to bring out the character of the various personages in the

play. Compare the treatment and relative importance of the strike in this play and in Galsworthy's "Strife." Was Galsworthy interested in the strike more as a social phenomenon or only as a means of drawing characters, who are set in motion *by* the strike? What use has Miss Sowerby made of the strike?

4. Study the construction of the second act. In what way is the action brought to a climax? Is this act in accordance with the formula of the well-made play?

Is the incident of Martin and Janet pertinent to the main idea? What is its dramatic reason for being? Could it have been omitted without harming the play as a whole?

5. Does young John's speech (p. 30) about Moloch seem out of place? That is, does the old-fashioned "raisonneur" method of exposing ideas harmonize with the decidedly realistic tone?

ELIZABETH BAKER

Elizabeth Baker was born in London. Starting her
life as a cashier, she learned shorthand and typewrit-
ing and before long became a stenographer. At present she is a private secretary, and writes plays in her
leisure hours. Her first play—"Beastly Pride," a
short trifle, was produced at the Croyden Repertory
Theater, and was so well received that Miss Baker
was encouraged to write a full-length play. This was
"Chains," produced first by the Play Actors, then
at Charles Frohman's Repertory Theater (Duke of
York's), and has since been seen at most of the repertory theaters of Great Britain. An adaptation was
played in New York. "The Price of Thomas Scott"
was produced by Miss Horniman's Company in London and Manchester in 1913.

Like Miss Sowerby, Miss Baker was an amateur—
in the true sense: she wrote plays because she liked
to write them, with little or no hope of their being
professionally produced. Both these women have gone
to everyday life for their material, both have cared
and dared to write about dull, ordinary people. In
Miss Baker's case this is especially true. "Chains"
is the simple picture of the clerk class, pathetic and
dispassionate. Her sincerity, her simplicity, her
power of analysis, her penetration, entitle her to a

place among the very few writers in England to-day whose work is sincere and significant.

PLAYS

BEASTLY PRIDE (1907).

CHAINS (1909).

Performed, in adapted form, at the Criterion Theater, New York 1913.

MISS TASSEY (1910).

CUPID IN CLAPHAM (1910).

EDITH (1912).

THE PRICE OF THOMAS SCOTT (1913).

" Chains " is published by Luce; " Miss Tassey " by Sidgwick and Jackson (London); " The Price of Thomas Scott " by the same.

REFERENCE: William Archer, " Playmaking " (Small, Maynard).—*Magazine: Bookman,* vol. xxxvi (p. 640), vol. xxxii (p. 136).

CHAINS

A play in four acts. First performed in 1909.

Nothing can make clearer the great gulf between
the drama of to-day and the drama of yesterday than
a comparison of a Pinero play with " Chains." Miss
Baker's quiet unpretentious picture is the direct antithesis to the color, movement, and intrigue of " The
Gay Lord Quex." If Pinero was limited, as to technic
as well as to idea, so is Miss Baker, but each has
fulfilled an important function: Pinero brought the
artificial comedy of his predecessors to its height,
while Miss Baker has broadened the field of dramatic
endeavor.

1. In William Archer's " Playmaking " (pp.
48-9) the author, in speaking of what is dramatic
and what undramatic, refers to the present play:
" We have already seen, indeed, that in a certain type of play—the broad picture of a social
phenomenon or environment—it is preferable that
no attempt should be made to depict a marked
crisis. There should be just enough story to
afford a plausible excuse for raising and for lower-
ing the curtain. . . . As a specimen, and a successful specimen, of this new technic, I may cite
Miss Elizabeth Baker's very interesting play,

' Chains.' There is absolutely no ' story' in it, no
complication of incidents, not even any emotional
tension worth speaking of. . . . A city clerk,
oppressed by the deadly monotony and narrowness
of his life, thinks of going to Australia—and
doesn't go: that is the sum and substance of the
action. Also, by way of underplot, a shopgirl,
oppressed by the deadly monotony and narrowness
of her life, thinks of escaping it by marrying a
middle-aged widower—and doesn't do it. If any
one had told the late Francisque Sarcey or the late
Clement Scott, that a play could be made out of
this slender material, which should hold an audience absorbed through four acts, and stir them to
real enthusiasm, these eminent critics would have
thought him a madman. Yet Miss Baker has
achieved this feat, by the simple process of sup-
plementing competent observation with a fair
share of dramatic instinct."

Exactly what does the dramatist supply in
place of the usual dramatic clash? Does the struggle take place entirely within the minds of the
characters? Is " Chains " in any way a " well-
made " play? How?

2. The Russian dramatist Andreyeff is another
who believes that external incidents—" action "—
are not necessary for a play. In his " Letter on
the Theater " (quoted in the introduction to the
Scribner volume of translations) he asks the ques-

tion: " Is action, in the accepted sense of movements and visible achievements on the stage, necessary to the theater? " Andreyeff's plays for the greater part depict mental and spiritual struggles, but Andreyeff makes use of soliloquy and even has recourse to the *Deus ex machina* device of the ancients, by using such characters as " The Being in Grey " (in " The Life of Man ") to explain the thoughts of his characters. Miss Baker, who doubtless has no definite theories, however, allows her simple and eminently human characters to work out their own destiny, without the aid of outside explanation.

Compare the " static " plays, " The Intruder " of Maeterlinck and " The Life of Man " of Andreyeff, with " Chains."

JAMES BARRIE

Sir James Barrie was born at Kirriemuir in 1860. Receiving his education at Dumfries and Edinburgh University, he turned to journalism, pursuing his work first at Nottingham and later in London. Although he began the writing of novels and sketches at an early age, his plays were written contemporaneously, the first appearing in 1891.

Barrie is a novelist whose best plays show nothing of the methods of the novelist; he is more successful in this respect than his nearest competitor, Galsworthy. He is a born novelist and a born dramatist, the rarest of combinations. That same charm which emanates from "Sentimental Tommy" and "The Little Minister" has been carried over into "Peter Pan" and "What Every Woman Knows." With an unerring sense of true and fitting dramatic style, a charming sensibility, a knowledge of the devices of dramatic technic, Barrie writes plays which are sure to outlast the great mass of plays of the day.

PLAYS

BECKY SHARP (1891).

IBSEN'S GHOST (1891).

RICHARD SAVAGE (1891).

WALKER, LONDON (1892).

Performed at the Herald Square Theater, New York 1894.

JANE ANNIE (1893).

THE PROFESSOR'S LOVE STORY (1894).

Performed at the Star Theater, New York 1894.

THE LITTLE MINISTER (1897).

Performed by Maude Adams on tour 1897 and later.

THE WEDDING GUEST (1900).

QUALITY STREET (1902).

Performed by Maude Adams on tour 1903. Revived at Empire Theater, New York 1913.

THE ADMIRABLE CRICHTON (1902).

Performed, with William Gillette, at the Lyceum Theater, New York 1904.

LITTLE MARY (1903).

Performed at the Empire Theater, New York 1904.

PETER PAN (1904).

Performed by Maude Adams on tour 1906 and in revival 1913.

PANTALOON (1905).

Performed at the Criterion Theater, New York 1905-6.

ALICE-SIT-BY-THE-FIRE (1905).

Performed by Ethel Barrymore on tour 1905-6.

JOSEPHINE (1906).

PUNCH (1906).

WHAT EVERY WOMAN KNOWS (1908).

Performed by Maude Adams at the Empire Theater, New York 1908 and on tour.

OLD FRIENDS (1910).

THE TWELVE-POUND LOOK (1910).

Performed by Ethel Barrymore on tour 1911-2.

A SLICE OF LIFE (1910).

Performed by Ethel Barrymore at the Empire Theater, New York 1912.

ROSALIND (1912).

THE LEGEND OF LEONORA (1913).

Performed by Maude Adams on tour 1913-4.

THE WILL (1913).

Performed in New York 1913.

"DER TAG," OR THE TRAGIC MAN (1914).

"Walker, London" is published by Samuel French; "Quality Street" and "The Admirable Crichton" by Doran; "The Twelve-pound Look," "Pantaloon," "Rosalind," and "The Will" in a volume called "Half-Hours," by Scribner; "Der Tag" by same publisher.

(As "The Admirable Crichton," Barrie's best published play, is obtainable only in a $5.00 édition de luxe, two of the short plays are here selected for study.)

REFERENCES: P. P. Howe, "Dramatic Portraits" (Kennerley) and "The Repertory Theater" (Kennerley); William Archer, "Playmaking" (Small, Maynard); Brander Matthews, "A Study of the Drama" (Houghton Mifflin); A. B. Walkley, "Drama and Life" (Brentano).—*Magazines: Harper's Weekly,* vol. 1 (p. 272); *Fortnightly,* vol. lxxxv (p. 920); *Critic,* vol. xlviii (p. 334); *Current Literature,* vol. xl (p. 409), vol. xl (p. 524); *Forum,* vol. xli (p. 137); *Bookman,* vol. xxxii (p. 308), vol. xxxviii (p. 263); *Literary Digest,* vol. xlix (p. 643); *Century,* vol. lxxxviii (p. 801).

PANTALOON

A play in one act. First performed in 1905.

This fantasy is very different in spirit from " The Twelve-pound Look," although the technic, the charming stage-directions, the ever-present Barrie charm, bring the two into close relation.

1. The stage-directions are much fuller than those in " The Twelve-pound Look." This little fairy-tale must have a more elaborate setting, and the author spares no pains to make us well acquainted with all the facts. So full are these directions, that the play is practically a story, yet, in spite of this, the piece is more charming and effective as a stage piece than it would be as a short story. There are no irrelevancies.

Barrie feels so kindly toward his audience that he wishes to establish an intimate rapport with them. In " Peter Pan," Peter at one place comes forward to the public and begs them to applaud. (In principle this is the vaudeville method of establishing relations between the stage and " the house "). In " Pantaloon " Barrie repeats the trick. On page 16 Pantaloon says: " But you do think me funny, don't you, Fairy? Neither of you can look at me without laughing, can you? Try, Boy; try, Fairy. (*They try, but fail. He is moved.*) Thank you both, thank you kindly. If the public only knew how anxiously we listen for the laugh they would be less grudging of it." These words are, of course, put into the mouth of an old actor, but the device is none the less a personal touch of the dramatist's, introduced for the purpose above referred to.

2. In the same volume with " Pantaloon " and " The Twelve-pound Look " is another one-act play, " The Will." This is divided into three scenes. Does the technic of this last play differ widely from that of the other two—the present and the one about to be considered?

THE TWELVE-POUND LOOK

A play in one act.   First performed in 1910.

Perhaps the best way to test the ability of the novelist who is at the same time a dramatist is to ask
whether a certain play is better as a drama than it
would be as a novel or a story.   " The Twelve-pound
Look " might have been a story, but it is assuredly
better as a play, because the dramatist has by means
of externals, as a result of his own process of visualization, made points which could not have been so
effectively made had the story been cast into narrative form.   This is his justification.   This little piece
is not a novelized story: it is a play.

1. The question of stage-directions in modern
plays is an interesting and a curious one.   Bernard
Shaw went far to incorporate long and detailed
descriptions not only of settings but of states of
mind; he added irrelevant suggestions and ex-
planations, occasionally, it must be admitted, quite
outside the province of the *mere* dramatist.

Until very recently, Barrie has refused to print
his plays; one reason for this was that, since they
were written to be produced, much of the charm
and atmosphere would be lost if the dialogue were
reduced to cold type.   Finally, however, he has

found a way of creating this necessary atmosphere: the stage-directions in his few printed plays supply the much-feared deficiency, and it is to be doubted whether the imaginative reader loses much by not seeing the plays on the stage. Because of their whimsical charm, their personal intimacy, and literary merit, the stage-directions of Barrie surpass those of Shaw and Barker. Take, for example, the opening of " The Admirable Crichton ":

A moment before the curtain rises the Hon. Ernest Woolley drives up to the door of Loam House in Mayfair. There is a happy smile on his pleasant, insignificant face, which presumably means that he is thinking of himself. He is too busy over nothing, this man about town, to be always thinking of himself, but, on the other hand, he almost never thinks of any other person. Probably Ernest's great moment is when he wakes of a morning and realizes that he really is Ernest, for we must all wish to be that which is our ideal. We can conceive him springing out of bed light-heartedly and waiting for his man to do the rest. He is dressed in excellent taste, with just the little bit more which shows that he is not without a sense of humor: the dandiacal are often saved by carrying a smile at the whole thing in their spats, let us say. . . .

Throughout the play now under discussion there is a great deal of such intimate detail, but it will be noticed that, even if the dramatist describes something which cannot actually be seen on the stage, there is no irrelevancy. Every word makes for unity—in the reader's mind, if not for the spectator's physical eye. Can as much be said, for instance, of Shaw's " Getting Married "?

2. Barrie is a master of the one-act play-form. Does his technic differ radically from that of Sudermann in " Fritzchen "? Compare these two, then the present play with Shaw's " The Shewing-up of Blanco Posnet."

3. How far is " The Twelve-pound Look " intended to be realistic?

JOHN OSWALD FRANCIS

John Oswald Francis was born in 1882 at Merthyr
Tydfil, in South Wales. His early education was received in the neighborhood of his native town; after-
ward he attended the University College of Wales.
He then taught school: in Paris, in Wales, and, since
1907, in London. Francis began his literary career
a few years ago with contributions to *The College
Magazine,* and has since " dabbled in journalism " in
London. " Change " was his first full-length play;
it brought its author considerable renown, as it won
the Welsh Drama Competition in 1912, instituted by
Lord Howard de Walden.

Francis is here included first because of the intrinsic
value of his play, then because he is a true representative of the new Welsh movement in drama. In 1914
Lord Howard de Walden subsidized the Welsh National Drama Company, a repertory theater for plays
both in Welsh and English. As yet, " Change " is
the only play that has attracted widespread attention,
but the movement is, according to all indications,
thriving.*

* In a letter to the writer, Francis says: " . . . I believe in the music-hall and have no sympathy with the
'high-browed' condemnation of the people's joys. It is
one of my ambitions to write short plays, which, while
maintaining as high a literary merit as possible, will yet

PLAYS

CHANGE (1912).

Performed at the Booth Theater, New York 1914.

THE BAKE-HOUSE (1913).

THE POACHER.

FOR FRANCE (1914).

"Change" is published, with an introduction by Montrose J. Moses, in the "Drama League Series" (Doubleday, Page); "The Poacher" is published by Sidgwick and Jackson (London).

REFERENCE: Introduction to "Change."—*Magazines: Bookman,* vol. xxxix (p. 62); *Review of Reviews,* vol. li (p. 119).

appeal to the man in the street. . . . I was annoyed by some critic who, after 'Change,' called me 'this sad and somber realist.' By disposition, I am neither sad nor somber, and, on the strength of one play, whose sadness was dictated by the theme, it was not fair to envelop me in a mantle of perpetual black. When 'Change' went into the repertory for Wales, I wrote 'The Poacher' in order, amongst other things, to correct the notion that I did not like a bit of fun as much as anybody else."

CHANGE

A play in four acts. First performed in 1913.

"Change" was first produced in London by the Incorporated Stage Society in 1913, but when, a few months later, it was performed at Cardiff by the Welsh National Drama Company, it was, in the author's words, the first "performance in Wales of a Welsh play by a professional repertory company in the history of the country." As Mr. Moses remarks in his preface to the American edition of the play, "Change" shows "a realization of all that is significant in the modern spirit settling over Wales." As a play it is intrinsically significant as regards technic and idea.

1. The very title of this play puts it in the same class with "Magda," "Milestones," "Rutherford and Son," "The Younger Generation," and the other plays which are based upon the struggle between generation and generation, between what is new and what is old and established.

What is the "change" referred to in the title, and in what way has the dramatist made use of his material?

2. This play serves as an excellent illustration of the fact that time-worn stage conventions can be used in such a way as not to seem out of place or insincere. It is only when insincere construction and insincere characters are placed in a thoroughly conventional framework that conventional tricks and devices are offensive. Attention is called in the introduction (p. xv) to the mob scene outside, toward the end of the third act. This is unquestionably a trick, but so well is it handled, and so earnest is the author, that the scene somehow is not immediately reminiscent.

3. Many—it is safe to say, most—plays narrow down in the penultimate act to one, two, or three characters: one by one the subordinate characters are eliminated, so that when the climax comes, it can be all the more dramatic, because it rests on that " spire of meaning " of which Galsworthy speaks (p. 131). The reason for this is psychological: the law of attention demands that we fix our interest and sympathy on one object, for the presence of any more than one tends to scatter the attention. It is impossible to sympathize unless we can see individuals, or better still one individual, struggling with opponents. For two acts, " Change " has interested because of the theme, because of the numerous and varied characters, but rarely has our sympathy been aroused

for *persons;* in order to introduce the human element, Francis drove home his theme by showing us the mother and Lizzie Ann. No amount of mere talk could so move us as this last scene of the third act:

Gwen.—He's climbing the wall by Roberts's house. He's shouting to them. Lewis! Lewis! Go down! (*She bends forward, and gives a frightened shriek.*) There's our Gwilym. Look! He's on the wall, trying to pull Lewis away——

Lizzie Ann.—There's four soldiers. O Dduw! Don't look! Don't look! They're going to shoot!

(*She drags Gwen away from the window. There is a sound of firing without, followed by deep silence. In a whisper.*)

They've done it!

Gwen (*pointing to the window*).—Look!

Lizzie Ann (*shuddering*).—I can't.

Gwen.—You must.

Lizzie Ann.—I can't.

(*Gwen wavers a moment, and then forces herself toward the window and looks out.*)

Gwen.—They're carrying some one into Roberts's house. It's Lewis. No, there's Lewis! (*She bends forward; then in a harsh voice*) Lizzie Ann, come here!

(*Lizzie Ann goes quickly to her, and looks out. She starts and turns away, sobbing out, " Oh, machgen bach-i! "*)

Gwen.—Is it Gwilym?

Lizzie Ann.—Yes. Gwilym!

(*For a moment Gwen stands swaying to and fro.
Then, with a cry of anguish, she falls prostrate on
the floor.*)

Another proof that dramatists must *show* human
emotions in order to make their audiences *feel*.
Without this human element, it is doubtful whether
" Change " would be in any way a successful stage
play.

4. Compare the treatment of strikes in
" Change," " Strife," and " Rutherford and Son."

THE IRISH DRAMA

WILLIAM BUTLER YEATS

William Butler Yeats was born in Dublin in 1865. He is the son of John B. Yeats, the artist. His early education was received in his native city and in London. Early in his career he identified himself with numerous attempts to revive the legends and literature of ancient Ireland; in this connection his most important activity was the foundation, together with Lady Gregory, Edward Martyn, and George Moore, of *The Irish Literary Theater*. Yeats has spent many years in collecting folk-lore; this he has utilized in many of his plays and collected into volumes of prose essays. Outside his dramatic work, essays and collections of legendary material, are his poems, undoubtedly that part of his total output by which he will be longest remembered: " Poems," first and second series, " The Wanderings of Oisin," " The Secret Rose," and " The Wind Among the Reeds."

" The future will look back to Mr. Yeats as to a landmark in the literary history of Ireland, both because of his artistic achievement and because he has been a leader in a remarkable movement. Through his poetry the Celtic spirit moves like a fresh wind," says H. S. Krans, in his " William Butler Yeats." Yeats brought to the theater great poetic gifts, he went far to arouse interest in the past glory of his country; as propagandist, as manager, as lecturer, he

has done more than any other, with the possible exception of Lady Gregory, to create a new and living
art for Ireland, but he cannot be accounted a great
dramatist. His vision is too limited, his genius too
delicate, his temperament too subjective, to allow him
to stand aloof and let his characters work out their
destiny as human beings.

PLAYS

THE LAND OF HEART'S DESIRE (1894).
　　Performed at Wallack's Theater, New York 1901.
THE COUNTESS CATHLEEN (1899).
　　Performed at Madison Square Garden, New York
　　1905.
DIARMUID AND GRANIA (in collaboration with George
　　Moore, 1901).
KATHLEEN NI HOULIHAN (1902).
　　Performed at the Hudson Theater, New York 1905.
A POT OF BROTH (1902).
THE HOUR-GLASS (1903).
　　Performed at the Hudson Theater, New York 1904.
THE KING'S THRESHOLD (1903).
THE SHADOWY WATERS (1904).
ON BAILE'S STRAND (1904).
　　Performed at the Little Theater, Chicago 1911.
DEIRDRE (1906).
THE UNICORN FROM THE STARS (in collaboration with
　　Lady Gregory, 1907).
THE GOLDEN HELMET (1908).
　　There are a great many editions of Yeats's plays,
owing to the fact that the poet has in some cases

revised and rewritten certain of them six or seven times. The largest collected edition is that published by A. H. Bullen, at Stratford-on-Avon: " The Collected Works in Verse and Prose of William Butler Yeats " (in eight volumes. Macmillans publish a volume of his poetic plays in " Poetical Works," Vol. II). " The Land of Heart's Desire " is also published separately by Mosher (Portland, Maine). " Kathleen ni Houlihan," " The Hour-Glass," and " A Pot of Broth " are published in a single volume by Macmillan; " Kathleen ni Houlihan," " The Hour-Glass," and " The Unicorn from the Stars " are also published in a volume by the same; also " The Golden Helmet," in a volume with poems. " Diarmuid and Grania " has not been published.

" The Unicorn from the Stars " is a rewritten version of an earlier play, " Where There is Nothing," which is now out of print. " The Hour-Glass " is in " Chief Contemporary Dramatists " (Houghton Mifflin).

REFERENCES: Horatio Sheafe Krans, " William Butler Yeats and the Irish Literary Revival " (Doubleday, Page); Lady Gregory, " Our Irish Theater " (Putnam); Maurice Bourgeois, " John Millington Synge and the Irish Dramatic Movement " (Macmillan); Cornelius Weygandt, " Irish Plays and Playwrights " (Houghton Mifflin); Frank Wadleigh Chandler, " Aspects of Modern Drama " (Macmillan); B. Russell Herts, " Depreciations " (Boni, New York); Clayton Hamilton, " Studies in Stagecraft " (Holt); Ludwig Lewisohn,

"The Modern Drama" (Huebsch); George Moore, "Hail and Farewell" (Appleton); James Huneker, "The Pathos of Distance" (Scribner); W. B. Yeats, "Ideas of Good and Evil" (Macmillan); Alan Wade, "Bibliography of Yeats" ("Collected Works," Bullen, Vol. VIII); L. Paul-Dubois, "Contemporary Ireland" (Maunsel); anonymous, "The New Irish Drama," a reading list (Drama League of America). —*Magazines: Poet-Lore,* vol. xv (p. 83); *Critic,* vol. xliv (p. 26); *Collier's,* vol. xlviii (p. 15); *Living Age,* vol. cclxix (p. 655); *Fortnightly,* vol. xci (p. 342); *Harper's Weekly,* vol. xlviii (p. 291); *Book News Monthly,* vol. xxii (p. 1024); *Westminster Review,* vol. clxxvi (p. 1); *North American,* vol. clxxv (p. 473); *Quarterly,* vol. ccxv (p. 219).

THE COUNTESS CATHLEEN

A play in five scenes. First performed in 1899.

It has already been stated that Yeats's greatest contribution to the movement he went so far to establish was not the plays he wrote for it, but his unfailing encouragement, his managerial ability, his propagandist endeavors. Yet his plays deserve consideration, as they are attempts at a new style of drama, not as to form but as to treatment of subject-matter, and literary style. This, of course, has very little to do with dramatic technic, but the study of these accessories is well worth while. In his preface to the second volume of the " Poetical Works " he says: " I have chosen all of my themes from Irish legend or Irish history, and my friends have made joyous, extravagant, and, as I am certain, distinguished comedy out of the common life of the villages, or out of a fantasy trained by the contemplation of that life and of the tales told by its firesides. This theater cannot but be more interesting to people of other races because it is Irish, and, therefore, to some extent, stirred by emotions and thoughts not hitherto expressed in dramatic form. . . ."

1. There is a mystical atmosphere in " The Countess Cathleen " which is comparable with the earlier plays of Maeterlinck. In what respects is

this play similar in technic to "The Intruder" or "Pelléas and Mélisande"? Are there any indications that Yeats was influenced by the Belgian?

2. In a note to his "Deirdre" (in the "Collected Works") Yeats says: "The principal difficulty with the form of dramatic literature I have adopted is that, unlike the loose Elizabethan form, it continually forces one by its rigor of logic away from one's capacities, experiences, and desires, until, if one have not patience to wait till it comes, there is rhetoric and logic and dry circumstance where there should be life." In this play are there evidences of this struggle of which the poet speaks? Where and of what sort are they? Does Yeats fall into conventional grooves?

Is there any special reason why the play should be divided into five scenes? Are there well-defined divisions in the play: exposition, development, climax, etc.?

3. As in Stephen Phillips's "Paolo and Francesca," there are many lyrical passages and short speeches which are of independent value and striking beauty, apart from the dramatic context. Is

> "You shall at last dry like dry leaves, and hang
> Nailed like dead vermin to the doors of God,"

more effective because it is spoken by Maire in a certain place in this play, than it would be if it stood alone or as part of an epic? Are the superb lines,

> " The years like great black oxen tread the world,
> And God the herdsman goads them on behind,
> And I am broken by their passing feet."

epic or dramatic?

4. Read Yeats's " Kathleen ni Houlihan," a prose play which is eminently effective on the stage. Compare it carefully with " The Countess Cathleen." In what respects do the two plays differ? Why is the prose piece more " theatrical "? In " Kathleen ni Houlihan " are there any passages, as there are in " The Countess Cathleen," which might stand alone by reason of their intrinsic beauty?

5. Notice the stage-directions. They are simple, but they indicate the poet's sense of action and dramatic effect. The play closes with: " *A sound of far-off horns seems to come from the heart of the Light. The vision melts away, and the forms of the kneeling PEASANTS appear faintly in the darkness.*" Often a dramatist throws out a hint, which the stage-manager is intended to act upon, filling in the necessary " business." How much leeway has the manager in the present play?

JOHN MILLINGTON SYNGE

Edmund John Millington Synge was born at New-town Little, in the vicinity of Dublin, in 1871. Not much is known of his early life, except that he lived at home until he was nearly twenty, that he entered Trinity College, Dublin, in 1888, and was graduated four years later. His predilection was for languages and music, although he was ever an ardent nature-lover. For many years he wandered about the Continent, writing a little and allowing impressions of men and nature to gather in his receptive mind. He went first to Germany, with the intention of pursuing his musical studies; after a year, he abandoned the idea and went to Paris, in order to do literary criticism. Still uncertain of his true calling, he made various though unsuccessful attempts to write poetry and essays. He did not " find himself " until he was dis-covered by another young enthusiast from Ireland, W. B. Yeats, who, in 1898, induced him to leave Paris and return to Ireland and devote himself to a study of the people, and write real Irish plays for the recently-founded Irish Theater. In the Aran Islands, in Wicklow and Kerry and Connemara, Synge found the necessary material and inspiration for his plays. He died of cancer at Dublin in 1909.

Synge was quiet, introspective, reticent, yet he al-lowed his true temperament—with all its wild vagarious longings, its furious exultations—to find expression in his plays. " He loves," says Yeats, " all that has edge, all that is salt in the mouth, all that is rough to the hand, all that heightens the emotions by contest, all that stings into life the sense of tragedy. . . . The food of the spiritual-minded is sweet, an Indian scripture says, but passionate minds love bitter food." His interest was in humanity, in everyday life, especially in those manifestations of primitive life which he knew so well how to seek out and use to advantage.

PLAYS

THE SHADOW OF THE GLEN (1903).

Performed by the Irish Players on tour 1912-3.

RIDERS TO THE SEA (1904).

Performed by the Irish Players on tour 1912-3.

THE WELL OF THE SAINTS (1905).

Performed by the Irish Players on tour 1912-3.

THE PLAYBOY OF THE WESTERN WORLD (1907).

Performed by the Irish Players on tour 1912-3.

THE TINKER'S WEDDING (1909).

DEIRDRE OF THE SORROWS (1910).

Performed by the Chicago Musical College 1913.

" The Works of John M. Synge," a collected edition in four volumes, is published by Luce. Cheap editions of all the plays are published separately by the same publisher. " Riders to the Sea " is included in " Chief Contemporary Dramatists " (Houghton Mifflin). Maunsel publishes the complete plays in one volume.

REFERENCES: Francis Bickley, " J. M. Synge and

the Irish Dramatic Movement" (Houghton Mifflin);
Maurice Bourgeois, "John Millington Synge and the
Irish Theater" (Macmillan); C. E. Montague,
"Dramatic Values" (Macmillan); P. P. Howe,
"J. M. Synge" (Kennerley); Cornelius Weygandt,
"Irish Plays and Playwrights" (Houghton Mif-
flin); George Moore, "Hail and Farewell" (Ap-
pleton); Lady Gregory, "Our Irish Theater" (Put-
nam); W. B. Yeats, "The Cutting of an Agate"
(Macmillan); L. Paul-Dubois, "Contemporary
Ireland" (Maunsel); Ludwig Lewisohn, "The
Modern Drama" (Huebsch); Clayton Hamilton,
"Studies in Stagecraft" (Holt); Darrell Figgis,
"Studies and Appreciations" (Dutton); William
Archer, "Playmaking" (Small, Maynard); John
Masefield, "Dictionary of National Biography";
Mario Borsa, "The English Stage of To-day"
(Lane); Frank Wadleigh Chandler, "Aspects
of Modern Drama" (Macmillan); James Huneker,
"The Pathos of Distance" (Scribner); John M.
Synge, prefaces to "The Playboy of the Western
World" and "The Tinker's Wedding"; "The Aran
Islands" and "In Kerry and Wicklow" (Luce).—
Magazines: Contemporary Review, vol. xcix (p. 470);
Dial, vol. l (p. 37), vol. liv (p. 233); *Living Age,* vol.
cclxix (p. 163), vol. cclxxx (p. 777); *Nation,* vol.
xciii (p. 376), vol. xcv (p. 608); *Yale Review,* vol. i
(p. 192), vol. ii (p. 767); *Forum,* vol. xlvii (p. 55);
Current Literature, vol. liii (p. 695).

RIDERS TO THE SEA

A play in one act. First performed in 1904.

This little drama, while it has none of the uproarious "romping" of "The Playboy," is still an unmistakable indication of Synge's keen enthusiasm for all that concerns human life. If he can take pleasure in the vitality and animal spirits of a Christy Mahon, he can likewise savor the dumb tragedy of a Maurya. The play is a picture, compressed and synthesized, of the helplessness of a mother in her hopeless struggle with the sea.

1. Synge's perfect mastery of words is one of his greatest assets. Like Shakspere, he can at once supply environment, create atmosphere, paint word-pictures. That sharp contrast between the homely and everyday in life and the gruesomeness of death is clearly drawn in "Riders to the Sea." Bartley says: "Where is the bit of new rope, Cathleen, was bought in Connemara?" and Cathleen replies: "Give it to him, Nora, it's on a nail by the white boards. I hung it up this morning, for the pig with the black feet was eating it." This is what Yeats means when he speaks of Synge's loving all that has edge.

2. In " Vale," the second volume of his " Hail and Farewell," George Moore wrote of " Riders to the Sea ": ". . . when I heard this one-act play, it seemed very little more than the contents of Synge's notebook, an experiment in language rather than a work of art, a preparatory essay; he seemed to me to have contented himself with relating a painful rather than a dramatic story, his preoccupation being to discover a style, a vehicle of expression. . . ." And the incident *is* painful rather than dramatic, for the struggle must be felt in the background, it cannot be seen and participated in by the audience. Consequently, we might almost feel that the struggle here depicted was so hopeless as to leave no room for anything but dumb submission. A true tragedy ought to give the hero a chance to fight; here the dice are loaded. The play is, however, a powerful and beautiful picture.

" Riders to the Sea " serves to illustrate the essential difference between the one-act play and the play in two or more acts: since the former is almost always concerned with but a single incident, it is capable of very little development. Now a tragedy is not a fact nor an event; it must show great and strong characters—or at least characters in which there is potential greatness or strength—struggling with forces which are finally too great to be overcome. And *we must see the struggle.* A tragic figure must have the opportunity to fail honorably, and we wish to see him trying to evade his fate. "Hamlet" would be ordinary melodrama if we were deprived of his soul-revealing soliloquies; "Œdipus," too, if we could not follow the King's efforts to escape what was decreed. A one-act play can scarcely more than indicate the result of a struggle. The last act of "Hamlet" is not a tragedy in itself, and "Riders to the Sea," like that last act, is but the result of what has gone on for a long time before. At the end we feel something of the great sorrow and eventual peace of the old woman in her last words: "Michael has a clean burial in the far north, by the grace of the Almighty God. Bartley will have a fine coffin out of the white boards, and a deep grave surely. What more can we want than that? No man at all can be living forever, and we must be satisfied." Still, the struggle was wanting.

Is a one-act tragedy possible?

THE PLAYBOY OF THE WESTERN WORLD

A comedy in three acts. First performed in 1907.

In the preface to " The Playboy " Synge wrote: ". . . in countries where the imagination of the people, and the language they use, is rich and living, it is possible for a writer to be rich and copious in his words, and at the same time give the reality, which is the root of all poetry, in a comprehensive and natural form." This play is the living embodiment of Synge's ideas on the combination of reality and poetry in the drama. " The Playboy "—indeed, all of Synge's plays—is outside the realm of literary " movements " and coteries; his plays are not plays of ideas. Theses and problems die. Ideas are for a generation, or for a few generations. Again the dramatist expounds (in the preface to " The Tinker's Wedding "): " The drama is made serious—in the French sense of the word—not by the degree in which it is taken up with problems that are serious in themselves, but by the degree in which it gives the nourishment, not very easy to define, on which our imaginations live. . . . The drama, like the symphony, does not teach or prove anything. . . ."

1. In his travel-book, " The Aran Islands," we find the following passage: ". . . He often tells

me about a Connaught man who killed his father
with the blow of a spade when he was in a passion,
and then fled to this island and threw himself on
the mercy of some of the natives. . . . They hid
him in a hole . . . and kept him safe for weeks,
though the police came and searched for him, and
he could hear their boots grinding on the stones
over his head. In spite of a reward which was
offered, the island was incorruptible, and after
much trouble the man was safely shipped to
America.

" This impulse to protect the criminal is universal in the west. It seems partly due to the association between justice and the hated English juris-
diction, but more directly to the primitive feeling
of these people, who are never criminals yet always
capable of crime, that a man will not do wrong
unless he is under the influence of a passion which
is as irresistible as a storm on the sea. If a man
has killed his father, and is already sick and broken
with remorse, they can see no reason why he should
be dragged away and killed by the law.

" Such a man, they say, will be quiet all the rest
of his life, and if you suggest that punishment is
needed as an example, they ask, ' Would any one
kill his father if he was able to help it? ' "

Out of his sympathy and enthusiasm for life, its
humor, its bite, its contradictions, its exhilaration,
Synge wrote this play. The dramatist's end was

" reality " and " joy." He was little concerned
with technic, he had no purpose but that of allowing his living creatures to revel in life, to revel in
rich idioms. Still, this apparently spontaneous
comedy was the result of arduous labor: George
Moore relates that the last act was rewritten thir-
teen times.

2. Many plays, of all ages and periods, have
contained first acts with very little in them but
the exposition of a few facts and the creation of
the environment or *milieu*. The opening of " The
Playboy " is full of atmosphere, and strikes the
keynote of the action which is to follow; but there
is no such conscious preparation as there is in the
expository act of Pinero's " Thunderbolt." Peg-
een Mike, in Synge's play, opens the act with:
" Six yards of stuff for to make a yellow gown. A
pair of lace boots with lengthy heels on them and
brassy eyes. A hat is suited for a wedding-day.
A fine tooth comb. To be sent with three barrels
of porter in Jimmy Farrell's creel cart on the evening of the coming Fair to Mister Michael James
Flaherty. With the best compliments of this season. Margaret Flaherty." Compare this simple
paragraph with the elaborate preparatory open-
ings of " The Second Mrs. Tanqueray " and
" Iris."

3. Throughout the play the development of the
plot, such as it is, goes hand in hand with the

development of Christy's character. Beginning with Christy's "I had it in my mind it was a different word and a bigger " (just after his entrance in the first act), trace, by reference to his speeches, how, in his own estimation and in that of his audience, he grows from " a slight young man . . . very tired and frightened and dirty " to a " likely gaffer in the end of all." There is a certain similarity between the growth of Hamlet's character and Christy's.

4. " The Playboy " is literary in the dramatic sense of the word. Can the same be said of Stephen Phillips's " Paolo and Francesca "?

AUGUSTA GREGORY

Lady Augusta Gregory was born at Roxborough, County Galway, Ireland, in 1859. For many years she has participated, like Yeats, in various revivals of Irish lore and literature, and in the creation of a national theater and drama. Together with Yeats and other collaborators, she helped found the *Irish National Theater Society,* and is now manager of the Abbey Theater in Dublin.

Lady Gregory is one of the most important figures in the modern Irish movement: her rewriting of the ancient Irish legends—in "Cuchulain of Muirthemne," "Gods and Fighting Men," and "The Book of Saints and Wonders"—her plays, her lecturing, her co-operation in innumerable societies for the social and political betterment of her country, entitle her to a place of honor by the side of Yeats. Her best plays, her comedies that is, were written in order to furnish relief to the historical plays, the folk and fairy-plays which were at one period threatening to make the Abbey Theater a one-sided institution. In the note appended to "Spreading the News," she says: "The idea of this play first came to me as a tragedy. . . . But comedy and not tragedy was wanted at our theater to put beside the high poetic work, 'The King's Threshold,' 'The Shadowy Waters,' 'On Baile's Strand,' 'The Well of the Saints'; and I let laughter

have its way with the little play." Five of the comedies in her volume called " Seven Short Plays," and
one or two others, are surely as quaint and humorous
and truly comic as any of our time. They may well
be compared with the lighter pieces of Molière: kindly
yet satirical, gay yet at times bitter, but always intensely human. Lady Gregory excels in the one-act
form; in her longer plays, like " The Image," she
lacks the necessary skill in the construction of a moving and interesting story. Of mystic and tragic beauty
Lady Gregory is more sparing, but " The Traveling
Man " and " The Gaol Gate," the latter in particular,
are noble bits of pathos, well written in stately and
rhythmical prose. Were it not for the haunting echoes
of Synge's language, there would be no ground for
hesitating to place Mary Cahel's speeches in " The
Gaol Gate " as the finest prose produced in the Irish
Theater.

PLAYS

SPREADING THE NEWS (1904).
    Performed by the Irish Players on tour 1911-2.
KINCORA (1905).
THE WHITE COCKADE (1905).
HYACINTH HALVEY (1906).
    Performed by the Irish Players on tour 1911-2.
THE GAOL GATE (1906).
    Performed by the Irish Players on tour 1911-2.
THE CANAVANS (1906).
THE JACKDAW (1907).
    Performed by the Irish Players on tour 1911-2.

THE RISING OF THE MOON (1907).

    Performed by the Irish Players on tour 1911-2.

THE POORHOUSE (in collaboration with Douglas Hyde, 1907).

DERVORGILLA (1907).

THE UNICORN FROM THE STARS (in collaboration with W. B. Yeats, 1907).

THE WORKHOUSE WARD (1908).

    Performed by the Irish Players on tour 1911-2.

THE IMAGE (1909).

    Performed by the Irish Players on tour 1911-2.

THE TRAVELING MAN (1910).

THE FULL MOON (1910).

COATS (1910).

    Performed by the Irish Players 1913.

THE DELIVERER (1911).

MACDARRAGH'S WIFE (1912).

THE BOGIE MEN (1912).

DAMER'S GOLD (1912).

    Performed by the Irish Players 1913.

    Lady Gregory has translated plays by Molière, Sudermann, and Goldoni.

    " Spreading the News," " Hyacinth Halvey," " The Gaol Gate," " The Jackdaw," " The Rising of the Moon," " The Workhouse Ward," and " The Traveling Man " are published in " Seven Short Plays " by Maunsel (Putnam is the American agent); " Grania," " Kincora," " Dervorgilla," " The Canavans," " The White Cockade," and " The Deliverer " are published by Putnam in two volumes as " Folk-History Plays "; " The Image " is published separately by Maunsel;

" The Full Moon," " Coats," " MacDarragh's Wife,"
" The Bogie Men," and " Damer's Gold " are published by Putnam in " New Comedies "; " The Rising
of the Moon " is included in " Chief Contemporary
Dramatists " (Houghton Mifflin). The translations
from Molière are published by Maunsel in " The Kil-
tartan Molière." The other translations are not published. For " The Unicorn from the Stars," see under
William Butler Yeats. " The Poorhouse " is not
obtainable.

REFERENCES: See under William Butler Yeats, general reference books on the Irish movement by Cornelius Weygandt, Mario Borsa, L. Paul-Dubois, Maurice
Bourgeois, Lady Gregory, W. B. Yeats, George
Moore, Clayton Hamilton, and Ludwig Lewisohn.—
Magazines: Quarterly Review, vol. ccxv (p. 234);
Collier's, vol. xlvii (p. 15); *Outlook,* vol. xcix (p.
916); *Forum,* vol. xlviii (p. 465); *Contemporary Review,* vol. cii (p. 602); *Independent,* vol. lxxiv (p.
857); *Living Age,* vol. cclxxxi (p. 332).

HYACINTH HALVEY

A comedy in one act. First performed in 1906.

The note (p. 205, " Seven Short Plays ") tells of
the origin of this little play: " I was pointed out one
evening a well-brushed, well-dressed man in the stalls,
and was told gossip about him, perhaps not all true,
which made me wonder if that appearance and behavior as of extreme respectability might not now and
again be felt a burden. After a while he translated
himself in my mind into Hyacinth; and as one must
set one's original a little way off to get a translation
rather than a tracing, he found himself in Cloon,
where, as in other parts of our country, ' charácter '
is built up or destroyed by a password or an emotion,
rather than by experience or deliberation. The idea
was more of a universal one than I knew at the first,
and I have had but uneasy appreciation from some
apparently blameless friends."

Like most of Lady Gregory's comedies, " Hyacinth
Halvey " contains a universal idea or basis: reputation is in a great measure a matter of " a password
or an emotion." Hyacinth, having a good reputation
thrust upon him, may do as he likes: his good name
will cling to him. In this play we laugh at humanity:
here is the essence of comedy.

1. In the realm of what is termed the modern drama, we have seen that classification is becoming more and more difficult. " Hyacinth Halvey " can safely be termed comedy, but comedy with a continual tendency toward farce. The characters are undoubtedly " possible," and the situation likewise, yet somehow Hyacinth's unbroken series of failures to lose his good reputation, and Fardy Farrell's unparalleled failures to lose his bad one, lead us to assume that the dramatist is bordering upon farce. Possibly the Irish setting and the good simple people render the episodes sufficiently foreign to enable us to accept the facts, yet these characters are so delightfully human that they must be taken as universal types.

2. This play, together with " Spreading the News," " The Jackdaw," and " The Workhouse Ward," raises again the question of comedy and tragedy. At the risk of being paradoxical, one might say that a tragedy is a play the closing of which is its goal, the spire of its meaning; a comedy is one the whole of which stands in and by itself, for the sake of its characters, and which *has no end*. Tragedy shows the struggles of strong individuals against fate (" Œdipus ") or circumstances (" Romeo and Juliet "); against themselves (" Hamlet ") or against others (" Julius Cæsar " and " Othello "), and *must end* in defeat. Comedy is not concerned with the outcome; it

amuses us from minute to minute: the outcome never seriously matters. Usually the end is the union of lovers, which is the merest convention. Had " Hamlet " ended in any other way than as it does, the play would have been spoiled or radically changed, had " As You Like It " not ended with the series of unions, the play would still have had meaning in itself, intrinsic dramatic value. Tragedy points forward to the catastrophe—it is not a tragedy until the tragic outcome occurs —comedy is sufficient unto itself.

Lady Gregory has recognized this fact, and has left three or four of her comedies with " hanging " ends. The best examples of this are " Hyacinth Halvey " and " The Jackdaw." In the former, we are shown Hyacinth trying in vain to undeceive the people as to his " charácter "; a series of incidents demonstrates the utter futility of the attempt. There is no *dénouement;* " Let us therefore ring down the curtain," says Lady Gregory.

Similarly, in " The Jackdaw," there is no solution: the police are coming, there will doubtless be an explanation, but that will not interest us. Therefore the dramatist says: " *Sounds of feet and talking and knock at the door. Cooney hides under counter. Nestor lies down on top of bench, spreads his newspaper over him. Mrs. Broderick goes behind counter.*" Then Nestor says: "(*raising paper from his face and looking out*) Tommy

Nally, I will give you five shillings if you will draw ' Tit-Bits ' over my feet."—That is the end.

3. Notice by way of comparison the elaborate *dénouements* of " Sweet Lavender " and " The Liars."

THE RISING OF THE MOON

A play in one act. First performed in 1907.

The origin of this little patriotic play was of the slightest sort, according to the author (see p. 205, "Seven Short Plays"). Its simplicity, its direct emotional appeal, its quiet humor, leave scarcely any ground for criticism or analysis.

1. With all its simplicity, "The Rising of the Moon" is a carefully prepared little play. Observe the methods used to create atmosphere. An effective bit of "living stage-direction" is the speech: "There's a flight of steps here that leads to the water. This is a place that should be minded well. If he got down here, his friends might have a boat to meet him; they might send it in here from outside." Without more ado, the action is begun: two and a half pages supply what preparation is needful, then the Ballad-singer comes in. The quick, short dialogue, the quaint idioms, the amusing manner in which the slight plot winds about, but ever pursues its way upward to the climax (pp. 94-5)—all this reveals careful workmanship. The *dénouement* is brief, and the close very effective.

Could Lady Gregory have left the end of this

play "hanging," as she did in "Hyacinth Halvey" and "The Jackdaw"?

2. During the past few years certain critics and dramatists—Synge, Jones,* Bennett, and Knoblauch are among the latter—have either openly or in practice advocated a return to the play for the play's sake, and have consistently avoided thesis plays, plays with "ideas." Ideas, they feel, are usurping the place of joy and life in the theater. They object in general to Brieux and Bernard Shaw, not primarily because such dramatists write plays for the purpose of furthering a reform or combating a social abuse or setting forth problems, but because in so doing they are abusing the dramatic form, which is intended to represent all of life, and not to expose ideas which have to do, in a greater or less degree, with life.

Lady Gregory, in particular, depicts life as she sees it, and allows ideas to grow out of her portrayal of it. She is always more interested in people than in things and abstract ideas, so that her plays are likely to outlive those of Hervieu and Brieux in which abstractions preponderate. She is not devoid of ideas—far from it—only her ideas are always inseparable from her characters. She has not "lost sight of the individual."

3. In what respects is "The Rising of the Moon" a theatrical play?

* See Henry Arthur Jones, "The Theater of Ideas" (Doran).

T. C. MURRAY

T. C. Murray was born in a small town in the County Cork, in 1873. Educated at local schools, he entered St. Patrick's College in Dublin, and studied to become a teacher. At the end of two years, he was qualified to teach as a National schoolmaster, and has taught in various schools in his native county. At an early age he wrote verse, and in 1909 his first play, " The Wheel o' Fortune," was produced at a little theater in Cork.

Extracts from a letter to the writer will explain some of Mr. Murray's activities: " I think I may at the outset safely describe myself as a playwright by accident. Five or six years ago a knot of Cork people of literary tastes formed a society for the production of original plays by Corkmen. The secretary buttonholed me on the street one Saturday evening, desiring to know if I had ever essayed anything in drama. I had not. . . . He urged me to try something in dramatic literature for the society and in a few weeks the MS. of ' The Wheel o' Fortune,' a little one-act comedy of matchmaking, was in his hands. . . . The comedy, despite its many crudities, proved a surprising success. Something over a year ago I reconstructed the ending . . . and rewrote most of the dialogue, and it was produced by the Abbey Company . . . under the title of ' Sovereign

Love.' ' Birthright' (October, 1910) followed ' The Wheel o' Fortune.' Whatever craft there is in it comes from pure instinct. After ' Birthright' came ' Maurice Harte' (June, 1912), and in the meantime I had devoured all that was significant in modern dramatic literature, making a study of the Russian, Norwegian, Swedish, and German schools of drama . . . I am told that the technic of ' Maurice Harte' is inferior to that of ' Birthright.' Instinct itself proved the surer guide in shaping and working out my theme! "

PLAYS

THE WHEEL o' FORTUNE (1909).
BIRTHRIGHT (1910).
Performed by the Irish Players on tour 1911-2.
MAURICE HARTE (1912).
Performed by the Irish Players on tour 1912-3.
SOVEREIGN LOVE (1914).

" Birthright " and " Maurice Harte " are published by Luce. The other plays have not yet appeared in print.

REFERENCES: Books already referred to by Cornelius Weygandt, Frank Wadleigh Chandler, Clayton Hamilton.

BIRTHRIGHT

A play in two acts. First performed in 1910.

" Birthright " is unquestionably the best of the realistic plays of the younger generation of Irish playwrights. It is masterly in construction, full of good characterization, and contains the spirit of true tragedy. No other Irish play of its kind is so relentlessly direct, so moving, so stirring and powerful. Like the same author's " Maurice Harte," it is concerned with a family struggle: the conflict between man and wife, between brother and brother.

1. The dialogue of the first fifteen pages appears casual and yet inevitable. While this is all exposition, at the same time it starts an emotional rise. The antagonism of Bat and his wife Maura is clearly set forth in words and action, while that between the brothers, neither of whom has yet appeared, is introduced in the course of the conversation. Then Shane, the younger son, comes in (p. 15). There is a momentary release of dramatic tension, then a foreboding note in the remarks about the weather (see paragraph on the " pathetic fallacy," p. 156, present volume), then the elder son, Hugh, makes his appearance (p. 19). Here is a striking contrast, for Hugh is a

splendid, athletic, whole-hearted fellow. The scene
with his mother affords contrast as well as necessary information for the audience. Hugh must go
out for the evening; he leaves just before his
father and brother re-enter. Again the fate-motif
is sounded: "Well, 'tis the long lane that have
no turning, and my brave Hugh have come to
the turning at last." For Bat has determined to
send Hugh to America in place of Shane (p. 27).
There is *a* climax at the end of this act, as Shane's
name on the trunk tag is changed to Hugh's. The
curtain leaves the audience just sufficiently sure of
what is to happen to avoid confusion, and curious
enough to feel further interest.

2. The first act has been analyzed in some detail
as to the progress of the story. One of the most
striking and admirable qualities of this play is
what may be termed sweep: compressed into two
short acts is a complete tragedy, the basis of
which is as old and as universal as the world.
Given the means and the background, the author
could scarcely have allowed more space to the development of the plot, and, judged according to
the criterion of theatrical effectiveness—or even
reading—it would have been superfluous and therefore fatal, to add more.

With very little preparation, the climax and
tragedy of the second act is reached: the first part
of the act is the simplest sort of development.

From the moment Shane enters (p. 38) the action rises swiftly, naturally, fatally, until Hugh is " felled to the ground," and the play closes.

Probably the extreme simplicity and directness of the play were the result of the author's instinctive feeling for what is dramatic. His words (p. 209) serve but to show that dramatists are for the most part born, not made.

3. St. John G. Ervine's " Mixed Marriage " is in four acts, yet its story is essentially as unified as that of " Birthright." In what way does Ervine justify the division into four, rather than three or two acts? Would " Mixed Marriage " have been a better play if it had been condensed into three acts, or two? Could it have been?

ST. JOHN G. ERVINE

St. John G. Ervine was born at Belfast, in 1883. He first entered the insurance business, then was dramatic critic of the *Daily Citizen*. Since his residence in London he has written a number of miscellaneous essays, a few plays, and the novel: " Mrs. Martin's Man."

Ervine is one of the younger group in the Irish movement, who, together with T. C. Murray and Lennox Robinson, have turned their attention to the realistic depiction of life in the cities and small towns. Ervine has with one exception laid the scene of his principal plays in and around Belfast: " Mixed Marriage," " The Orangeman," and " The Magnanimous Lover " are plays of town life, and stand in distinct contrast with the wild, half-imaginary fantasies of Synge, the quaint comedies of Lady Gregory, and the fairy twilight plays of Yeats. Ervine concerns himself with the struggle of character with character: Protestant and Catholic, youth and age, prejudice and freedom. His power lies in the creation of human characters. The father and mother in " Mixed Marriage," the father and mother again in " The Orangeman," and Jane Clegg in the play of that name, are distinct contributions. " Jane Clegg," his latest play, is laid in England, and marks a departure in subject-matter.

PLAYS

MIXED MARRIAGE (1911).

Performed by the Irish Players on tour 1911-2.

THE MAGNANIMOUS LOVER (1912).

THE ORANGEMAN (1913).

THE CRITICS (1913).

JANE CLEGG (1914).

ISA BLACKWOOD (1914).

The first four of these plays are published in a single volume, "Four Irish Plays," by Maunsel (Dublin); "Mixed Marriage" and "The Magnanimous Lover" are issued separately by the same publisher (Luce in America); "Jane Clegg" is published by Sidgwick and Jackson (London).

REFERENCES: Books already referred to under William Butler Yeats, by Cornelius Weygandt and Clayton Hamilton.—*Magazine: Everybody's,* vol. xxviii (p. 678).

MIXED MARRIAGE

A play in four acts. First performed in 1911.

This is primarily a play of character, the sort in which this dramatist excels. The men and women, and the environment in which they exist, are what interest him.

1. In order the better to set off his characters he has introduced a thesis, which is clearly stated (p. 7 of the "Four Irish Plays") in the first act. Rainey says: "A wudden have a son o' mine marry a Cathlik fur all the wurl. A've nathin' agin the girl, but A believe in stickin' t'yer religion. A Cathlik's a Cathlik, and a Prodesan's a Prodesan. Ye can't get over that." Tom replies: "Och, sure, they're all the same. Ye cudden tell the differs atween a Cathlik an' a Prodesan if ye met them in the street an' didden know what their religion wus. A'm not one fur marryin' out o' my religion meself, but A'm no bigot. Nora Murray's a fine wumman." With this plain statement of theme we might be prone to expect at first a thesis play, pure and simple, but the next speech affords at least a cue as to the trend the play will take. When Rainey declares, " Fine or no fine, she's a Cathlik an' A'll

niver consent til a son o' mine marryin' her," it is reasonable to assume that the play will be one of " conflicting wills." This is in fact what it is, and the wills conflict over a question which is after all of only secondary artistic importance. Rainey and Mrs. Rainey, Nora Murray and Hugh, must have something to struggle about, something which will develop and expose their characters.

This first act, like the succeeding ones, is well balanced: character against character, with sufficient plot and sufficient background to form an harmonious whole.

2. The struggle, it has been frequently observed, is one of the basic principles, though not unalterable laws, of the drama from time immemorial. A play in which there is a sharply indicated clash of interests, like Echegaray's " Madman or Saint " and the present work, begins with a more or less general statement: in the case of " Mixed Marriage " it consists in Rainey's objection to the intermarriage of Protestants and Catholics. First we are shown that his son Hugh is in love with Nora Murray, a Catholic. But the dramatist does not consider it sufficient to confine the struggle to these few people: he introduces external forces. Michael's words (p. 18) are ominous: " It mightn't be again you on'y though? " Notice how the struggle develops from the particular to the general.

THE AMERICAN DRAMA

BRONSON HOWARD

Bronson Croker Howard was born at Detroit, in 1842. Receiving his primary education in Detroit, he prepared himself for Yale at an eastern preparatory school, but was prevented from entering college because of an affection of the eyes. He then returned to Detroit, and joined the staff of the *Free Press*, to which he made numerous contributions. At the same time he was experimenting with the play-form. Most of his early attempts were never produced. His first play was a dramatization of an episode from "Les Misérables," called "Fantine"; this was produced in Detroit in 1864. The following year Howard came to New York, wrote for the *Tribune* and the *Post*, carried plays from manager to manager during a period of five years, until in 1870 Augustin Daly accepted and produced "Saratoga," which was immensely successful. From then on Howard's success was assured; "The Banker's Daughter," "Young Mrs. Winthrop," "The Henrietta," "Shenandoah," and "Aristocracy" were among the best-known and best-liked of American plays. Howard died at Avon-by-the-Sea, New Jersey, in 1908.

Brander Matthews (in "An Appreciation") says: "Bronson Howard's career as a dramatist covered the transition period of the modern drama when it was changing from the platform-stage to the picture-frame-stage. His immediate predecessor, Dion Boucicault, worked in accordance with the conditions of the platform-stage, with its rhetorical emphasis, its confidential soliloquies to the audience, and its frequent changes of scene in the course of the act. . . . When Bronson Howard began to write for the stage he accepted the convenient traditions of the time, although he followed T. W. Robertson in giving only a single scene to each act. As a result of this utilization of conventions soon to seem outworn, certain of his earlier plays appeared to him late in life incapable of being brought down to date, as they had been composed in accordance with a method now discarded. . . . He moved with his time; and his latest plays, 'Aristocracy' for one, and 'Kate' for another, are in perfect accord with the most modern formula. Yet he did not go as far as some other playwrights of to-day. He knew that the art of the theater, like every other art, can live only by the conventions which allow it to depart from the mere facts of life." Howard deserves the title of " Dean of American Drama " because he was the first to awaken to the fact that in the America of his day there was material for an indigenous drama, and he did his best, in spite of French influences, to throw off the conventions of the past and point a way to the future.

PLAYS

FANTINE (adapted from " Les Misérables," 1864).
SARATOGA (1870).
DIAMONDS (1872).

MOORCROFT (1874).

LILIAN'S LAST LOVE (1877).

THE BANKER'S DAUGHTER (revised version of "Lilian's Last Love," 1878).

OLD LOVE LETTERS (1878).

HURRICANES (1878).

WIVES (adapted from Molière, 1879).

FUN IN A GREEN-ROOM (1882).

YOUNG MRS. WINTHROP (1882).

ONE OF OUR GIRLS (1885).

MET BY CHANCE (1887).

THE HENRIETTA (1887).

BARON RUDOLPH (1887).

SHENANDOAH (1889).

ARISTOCRACY (1892).

PETER STUYVESANT (in collaboration with Brander Matthews, 1899).

KNAVE AND QUEEN (never acted).

KATE (never acted).

"Young Mrs. Winthrop" and "Saratoga" are published by French; "Kate" by Harper's; the other plays have not been published.

REFERENCES: "In Memoriam: Bronson Howard" (New York, 1910); "The Autobiography of a Play" by Bronson Howard, with an introduction by Augustus Thomas (Dramatic Museum of Columbia University); Montrose J. Moses, "The American Dramatist" (Little, Brown); Brander Matthews, "A Study of the Drama" (Houghton Mifflin); Richard Burton, "The New American Drama" (Crowell); Charlton Andrews, "The Drama To-day" (Lippincott).—*Maga-*

zines: Bookman, vol. x (p. 195), vol. xxviii (p. 55);
Century, vol. lxi (p. 28), vol. iii (p. 465); *Munsey,* vol.
xxxiv (p. 122, p. 199); *Theatre* (London), Aug.,1879;
Book Buyer, vol. xvi (p. 113); *Independent,* vol. lxi
(p. 735), and vol. lxv (p. 391); *North American,* vol.
clxxxviii (p. 504).

YOUNG MRS. WINTHROP

A play in four acts. First performed in 1882.

Of the three plays of Howard which have been published, " Young Mrs. Winthrop " is probably the best and most typical. The dramatist's best and worst qualities are easily discernible. Like some of his contemporaries and many of his followers, Howard possessed a great deal of that essential kindliness, sympathy with the weaknesses of human nature, and sentiment which permeate the American theater. " Young Mrs. Winthrop " is a kindly sermon on the dangers and blessings of matrimony, besides being an ingratiating and human, perhaps too " human," comedy.

1. Any play written in 1882 is likely to bristle with " asides," soliloquies, and other conventions which have since fallen into disfavor with dramatists. This play opens with a soliloquy:

Mrs. Ruth. (L.)—There, Miss Dolly! (*tying ribbon on the doll and holding it up*) you will have a beautiful mother to-morrow, and I shall be your grand-grandmother. Your name is to be ' Ruth '—after me —how do you like it? Your little mother has a very large family already, but I am sure she will love you more than any of the rest (*crosses to R. by fire, kisses the doll*). Lie here, my pet (*holding the doll to her breast*). You must go to sleep at once, for mother Rosie will be up very early in the morning. (*Enter Douglas*), etc.

A great deal of labor is spared the dramatist by allowing his audience to know (1) who the character present is, (2) what she is like, (3) a little of the situation. The first " aside " occurs on the next page (p. 4):

Doug. (*stopping. Aside*)—I asked Constance not to go to-night.

Again, an easy device. Then, on page 25, there is another soliloquy:

Enter Constance, up L.
Cons.—Back again! (*with a weary air, throwing aside her cloak. Pause*). How quiet the house is! It's no use going to bed; I cannot sleep. I wish these " social gaieties " as they call them, could go on forever. No matter how much I go out, or how bright the company is, it always ends in this; I am alone again, and I—I can't stop thinking. Oh!—I wish I *could!* I wish I could! Mr. Chetwyn was at the reception this evening. Douglas sent him word he could not meet him at the club. He sent the message after receiving that note from Mrs. Dunbar—*she* was *not* there to-night! Oh!—why must I keep thinking—

thinking? (*starting to her feet and moving C. Pauses*). Perhaps I am wronging him. Yes. No—no —I will *not* believe it—I *have* not lost his love! There is something I do not understand? I will speak to Douglas about it in the morning. (*Smiling.*) It will all come right. I must get to sleep as soon as I can, to be up bright and early with Rosie. I will peep in at my little darling before I go to sleep. (*Going toward door, R. 2 E.*)

It has often been said in defense of the " aside " and the soliloquy that since the drama is a series of conventions, why not accept these as well as that most necessary of conventions: the foreshortening of time? For over two thousand years these conventions have been accepted, why then should we cast them aside at this late date? The drama has changed radically during the past century, and is still developing at a rapid rate. With the change in subject-matter has come a corresponding change in manner of treatment: realistic subjects demanded realistic treatment. The " aside " is not natural, because it does not *seem* natural: people seldom or never turn their heads aside and utter words not intended to be heard by any one else; and when these words are spoken loudly enough to be overheard by a large audience, while the characters who must not hear them are within whispering distance of the speaker, the convention is too apparent. The uselessness of this particular convention is proved by the fact that almost every aside in a play can be deleted, and the audience be none the less well informed as to what is going on. Test this in the present play.

On the other hand, the soliloquy * is legitimate. Ibsen in " A Doll's House " has made generous use of it. People *do* soliloquize, often aloud; even if they did not, it is not unnatural to hear a character give voice to thoughts, which must be near the surface, when he is alone on the stage. Do Hamlet's soliloquies seem unnatural? Do Nora's in the Ibsen play just mentioned?

2. Howard's modernity of spirit, his vision of the path to be taken by the play of the future was incontestably greater than his actual achievement: he pointed out the way for those who were to be technically more efficient than he, for those who were, living in a later generation, to treat of questions of the day. Augustus Thomas says of him (in " The Autobiography of a Play "): " Some philosopher tells us that a factor of greatness in any field is the power to generalize, the ability to discover the principle underlying appar-

* " He [Bronson Howard] once said, half jokingly, to his collaborator in ' Peter Stuyvesant,' that, if he happened to write a play without a single soliloquy, he would be tempted to insert one, simply to retain the right to employ it when it was required. It may be noted, however, that he did not carry this out, since his last comedy, ' Kate,' is free from any soliloquy."—Brander Matthews in " An Appreciation " (" In Memoriam: Bronson Howard ").

ently discordant facts. Bronson Howard's plays are notable for their evidence of this power. He saw causes, tendencies, results. His plays are expositions of this chemistry. ' Shenandoah ' dealt broadly with the forces and feelings behind the Civil War; ' The Henrietta ' with the American passion for speculation—the money-madness that was dividing families. ' Aristocracy ' was a very accurate, although satirical, seizure of the disposition, then in its strongest manifestation, of a newly-rich and Western family of native force to break into the exclusive social set of New York and to do so through a preparatory European alliance."

What is the generalization in " Young Mrs. Winthrop "? Wherein lies its modernity?

3. Often—too often in the American drama—the child is brought into the action of a play in order to attract the sympathy of the audience. David Belasco has done this in " The Return of Peter Grimm " with notable effect. How has Howard utilized the child-motif in this play?

JAMES A. HERNE

James A. Herne was born in 1839 at Cohoes, New York. After receiving a very rudimentary education he left home at the age of twenty and joined a theatrical company in Troy, and began his actor's career in "Uncle Tom's Cabin." Soon after, he joined another company, played in Albany, then Baltimore, and at the age of thirty he became manager of the New York *Grand Opera House.* Leaving this situation, he became an actor again, and toured the country. His second marriage, in 1878, was a decisive point in his career: his wife, Miss Katherine Corcoran, helped and encouraged him to devote his time to the writing, rather than the acting of plays. His first play, "Hearts of Oak," was produced the year after his marriage. "Shore Acres," "Drifting Apart," "The Minute Men," "Sag Harbor," written during the next twenty years, brought their author fame and a good share of success. Herne continued to act for many years. He died in 1901.

Herne is a very important figure in American drama: in his melodramas there is a note of simplicity, of sympathy, of reality, which lifts them into the realm of true drama. In his most ambitious achievements, "The Rev. Griffith Davenport" and "Margaret Fleming," there was said to be "tragic sentiment," "forcefulness," and "serious simplicity."

Herne delighted and excelled in drawing rural types, and though he occasionally placed his characters in conventional settings and melodramatic situations, they were nearly always faithful and kindly portrayals of life. His technic was " old-fashioned," his ideas possibly antiquated, according to modern standards, but he was a force, an influence, an ideal.

PLAYS

HEARTS OF OAK (1879).
THE MINUTE MEN (1886).
DRIFTING APART (1888).
MARGARET FLEMING (1890).
SHORE ACRES (1892).
THE REV. GRIFFITH DAVENPORT (1899).
SAG HARBOR (1899).

None of Herne's plays has been published. In a fire that destroyed the Herne home in 1909, the MSS. of " The Rev. Griffith Davenport" and " Margaret Fleming " were lost.

REFERENCES: Montrose J. Moses, " The American Dramatist " (Little, Brown); Richard Burton, " The New American Drama " (Crowell); Norman Hapgood, " The Stage in America " (Macmillan); Charlton Andrews, " The Drama To-day " (Lippincott); Lewis C. Strang, " Famous Actors of To-day in America " (Page).—*Magazines: Arena,* vol. vi (p. 401), vol. viii (p. 304), vol. xvii (p. 361), vol. xxvi (p. 282); *Harper's Weekly,* vol. xliii (pp. 139, 213); *Literature,* vol. iv (p. 265); *Harper's Magazine,* vol. lxxxiii (p. 478); *National Magazine,* vol. xi (p. 393);

Pall Mall Magazine, vol. xx (p. 23); *Outlook,* Dec. 28, 1912; *Century,* vol. lxxxviii (p. 574).

NOTE.—Since there is no printed copy of any Herne play, it is inadvisable to include a study outline. For completeness' sake, however, and in case the play is ever published, there follow a few brief remarks on " Shore Acres."

SHORE ACRES

A play in three acts. First performed in 1892.

This play was, according to all accounts, an intensely " human," amusing, and, in places, exciting drama. The following quotations are illuminating; the first is from Montrose J. Moses's " The American Dramatist," the second from a letter by Henry George:

" Even in ' Shore Acres,' during the scene in which *Uncle Nat* struggles with *Martin* in his effort to light the signal lamp, the sensational is very much in evidence; but the unerring art of Mr. Herne saved him from the accusation of intense, glaring melodrama. He understood thoroughly the balance between tension and quietude, and there is no bit of stage writing more natural, more cheerful, and more real than the act which succeeded this violent one in ' Shore Acres,' *Uncle Nat* preparing the Christmas stockings. Those who are fortunate enough to recollect the wonderful naturalness of Mr. Herne's acting, will always point to the final curtain of this play, where *Uncle Nat*, left alone on the stage, by the very flexibility of his facial expression, depicted the full beauty of his character, as he closed up the room for the night, put out the lamps, and, lighted only by the glow from the fire in the stove, slowly left the room as the cuckoo clock struck twelve. Such work, of which Mr. Herne as an actor was capable, is to a certain extent the realization of Maeter-linck's idea of *static* drama."

" I cannot too much congratulate you upon your success. You have done what you sought to do—made a play pure and noble that people will come to hear. You have taken the strength of realism and added to it the strength that comes from the wider truth that realism fails to see; and in the simple portrayal of homely life, touched a *universal* chord. . . . Who, save you, can bring out the character you have created—a character which to others, as to me, must have recalled the tender memory of some sweet saint of God? "

AUGUSTUS THOMAS

Augustus Thomas was born at St. Louis, in 1859. He says (quoted in *The Outlook,* December 28, 1912): " After Farragut ran the New Orleans blockade my father took direction of the St. Charles Theater in New Orleans, then owned by Ben DeBar. When he returned to St. Louis in 1865, I was in my seventh year, and my earliest recollections are tinged with his stories of Matilda Herron, John Wilkes Booth, and others who played in that theater. Father was an orator of considerable ability, and I remember him reciting long speeches from Kotzebue, Schiller, and Shakspere. In his associations with the theater he took me very early to plays, and I have always been an attendant; consequently dialogue seemed the most natural literary vehicle. I found later that this impression was justified when I discovered that the most telling things in Homer and later Greek poets and philosophers were in dialogue—that this was true of Confucius and Christ. I began writing plays when I was about fourteen years of age. When I was sixteen and seventeen, an amateur company that I organized played in certain railway centers on the old North Missouri Railway for the benefit of local unions of the workingmen. In 1882 I made a dramatization of Mrs. Burnett's ' Editha's Burglar.' With this as a curtain-raiser and a rather slap-stick farce called

' Combustion,' I made a tour of the country with a company that I organized, and with which I ran in debt several thousand dollars. In 1889 a four-act version of ' The Burglar,' arranged by me, was played in New York and was successful, and since that time my royalties have enabled me to give my attention on the business side exclusively to play-writing."

Thomas is the most successful, skilful, and interesting of American dramatists of a former generation. Although he still writes plays, many of which have met with public approval, he belongs to the immediate past. "Arizona," a melodrama of the West, is one of his typical works; even "The Witching Hour," a later play, is notable for the very qualities which went to the making of the earlier melodrama. Thomas is ingenious, he knows well the art of contriving moving stories, he knows the taste of the public and the requirements of the actor; but his ideas, while they are occasionally very interesting, are not significant. He has little to do with characterization. He is important by reason of his cleverness, his zest in the externals of life.

PLAYS

EDITHA's BURGLAR (dramatization from a story by Mrs. Burnett, 1887).

A MAN OF THE WORLD (1889).

RECKLESS TEMPLE (1890).

AFTERTHOUGHTS (1890).

ALABAMA (1891).

IN MIZZOURA (1893).

THE CAPITOL (1894).

NEW BLOOD (1894).

THE MAN UPSTAIRS (1895).

THE OVERCOAT (1898).

THE HOOSIER DOCTOR (1898).

THE MEDDLER (1898).

OLIVER GOLDSMITH (1900).

ARIZONA (1900).

ON THE QUIET (1901).

COLORADO (1901).

SOLDIERS OF FORTUNE (1902).

THE EARL OF PAWTUCKET (1903).

THE OTHER GIRL (1903).

MRS. LEFFINGWELL'S BOOTS (1905).

DE LANCEY (1905).

THE EMBASSY BALL (1905).

THE RANGER (1907).

THE WITCHING HOUR (1907).

THE HARVEST MOON (1909).

THE MEMBER FROM OZARK (1910).

AS A MAN THINKS (1911).

THE MODEL (1912).

MERE MAN (1912).

INDIAN SUMMER (1912).

"Alabama" and "Arizona" are published by Sergel, Chicago; "The Witching Hour" by Houghton Mifflin in "Chief Contemporary Dramatists," and "As a Man Thinks" by Duffield.

REFERENCES: Montrose J. Moses, "The American Dramatist" (Little, Brown); Richard Burton, "The New American Drama" (Crowell); Charlton An-

drews, " The Drama To-day " (Lippincott); Arthur
Ruhl, " Second Nights " (Scribner); William Winter,
" The Wallet of Time," Vol. II (Moffat, Yard).—
Magazines: Collier's, vol. lxiv (p. 23); *Outlook,* vol.
xciv (p. 212); *North American,* vol. clxxxvii (p.
801); *Delineator,* vol. lxxiii (p. 221); *World's Work,*
vol. xviii; *Harper's Weekly,* vol. v (p. 13); vol. xliv
(p. 947); *Munsey,* vol. xxiv (p. 413); vol. xxvii (p.
522); *Bookman,* vol. xiv (p. 449), vol. xxxiii (p. 352);
Critic, vol. xliv (p. 205); *Sewanee Review,* April,
1907.

THE WITCHING HOUR

A play in four acts. First performed in 1907.

In common with Clyde Fitch, Alfred Capus, and
Sir Arthur Pinero, Augustus Thomas has always kept
abreast of the times in the matter of modes, customs,
and ideas. Probably his early journalistic career
taught him the value of being " alive," and he has
ever recognized the advantage of producing a play
the basic idea of which is in the public mind. It is
said that " The Witching Hour " was kept for ten
years " until the time was opportune." Montrose J.
Moses in his " American Dramatist " quotes Thomas
as saying: " ' The Witching Hour ' is a seizure of the
general attention that is given to telepathy and allied
topics. And under all that, lies my own theory, expressed on more than one occasion, that the theater
is a place for the visualizing of ideas—that the theater is vital only when it is visualizing some idea then
and at the time in the public mind. The theater is a
vital part of everyday life; it is an institution, and
as an institution it has a claim upon the popular
attention principally in that fact. When it becomes
a thing preservative, a museum for certain literary
forms, or a laboratory for galvanizing archaic ideas,
it is almost useless, and seldom successful as a business enterprise."

237

1. For a number of years Thomas has refused to allow the present play to appear in print; apart from certain practical reasons, he justly feared that a vehicle intended for production on the stage by actors, supported by scenery and " props " and lights, in which there was no attempt at " galvanizing archaic ideas," would not well survive the ordeal of being read. Very often good dialogue will suffer when perused in the library—dialogue that is interesting and effective on the boards; it is very doubtful whether George Cohan's " Get-Rich-Quick Wallingford " or " Broadway Jones " would be half so amusing in a book as they are in the theater. However, " The Witching Hour " may now be judged independently of the footlights.*

Few of the plays considered in the present vol-

---

* In an interview Augustus Thomas once said: " On the choice of words will depend very much the effectiveness of a play. The tone of them must change to suit the scene, the emotion. One way of creating humor is to use pompous or grandiloquent words. Emotion, on the other hand, keeps the words simple, very near the ground. Part of an audience might, perhaps, get deep feeling from unusual and very precise words, but the audience is made up for the greater part of people who are not thus trained. And when you write for the audience you must write for the great average. You will then use the simple, passionate words such as fire, stars, hand, heart, root, rock, grave. In the same way you may simplify your words by omitting many. For instance, note the increase in emphasis and force between, ' I wish you to go,' ' You must go,' ' Go !' and finally the simple opening of the door."

ume sound so natural, so "everyday" as this.
Note the very opening:

> *Jo.*—Massar Brookfield.
> *Jack (outside, left).*—Well, Jo?
> *Jo.*—Mr. Denning, sah.
> *Jack.*—Ask Mr. Denning to come up.
> *Jo.*—Yes, sah.
> (*Exit center. More talk and laughter, left.*)
> (*Jack enters left. . . .*)
> *Jack (at door, left).*—Lew! I say—Lew—you
> ladies excuse Mr. Ellinger a moment?
> *Helen, Alice, Viola (outside).*—Oh—yes. Cer-
> tainly.

Nothing could be more casual, yet there is an
underlying art—skilfully concealing itself—which
is typical of much of Thomas's best work. Rarely
does he attempt to be "literary," often he tries
to be the reverse, apparently through fear of being thought "literary." Compare this dialogue
with that of "Young Mrs. Winthrop" and of
"The Liars."

2. Thomas wished to write a play about tele-
pathic phenomena and superstition; and the exact
form into which he was to cast his play must have
suggested itself to him when he was thinking of
the incidents which would illustrate his ideas.
Since these situations would necessarily be of a
startling and novel nature, it seemed inevitable that
the play should fall into the category of melo-

drama. Telepathy is too new, the data are too scarce, to allow us to accept as matters of course Justice Prentice's " guessing " the price of the Corot (p. 330), or Clay's superstition about Tom's scarf-pin and the resultant murder (pp. 332-33). The melodramatic form was inevitable.

At what exact point in this first act are you aware that the play is to be a melodrama? What incident or incidents prove this?

3. " The Witching Hour " is thoroughly American in spirit: the good and bad qualities of American drama are easily distinguished from page to page. Generalizations in matters theatrical nowadays are especially fallible, yet it will not be amiss to say that the drama in the United States is as a rule conventional, over-sentimental, puritanical in that it rarely dares go to the root of life and comments on it with fearless and outspoken sincerity; it is, on the other hand, " live," moving, interesting as a transcript of the everyday externals of life. The dialogue is usually good, idiomatic, and clever, although it rarely reveals character. It is nearly always violent, extreme: melodrama and farce seem to be the favorite forms, and happy endings are practically indispensable. The American dramatist is a sentimentalist, although he seldom sentimentalizes over the deepest things in life—as a Frenchman does—love-scenes are usually short and " snappy "

—an American dislikes showing his feelings—
while little children, old mothers, and " pals " in
" crooked deals," supply more sentimental material than half a dozen love-affairs to a Frenchman
or a deserted mistress to Schnitzler.

Notice the first love-scene in " The Witching
Hour ": the actual proposal and its casual an-
nouncement (p. 323):

Clay.—Always you when I think about a real house,
you bet—a house for *me*—and you'll be there, won't
you? (*Takes her in his arms.*)
Viola.—Will I?
Clay.—Yes—say, " I will."
Viola.—I will.
(*Re-enter Alice and Helen.*)
Alice (astonished).—Viola!
(*Alice goes left.*)
Clay.—I've asked her—mother.
Alice.—Helen, you knew?
Helen.—Yes.
Clay (to Alice).—And I asked Jack, too.
Alice.—You mean——
Clay.—We're engaged—if you say it's all right.
Alice.—And you—Viola?
Viola (nodding).—Yes——

Here are the barest outlines; not a trace of
passion, and what feeling there is must be expressed by the actors. How different from the
long pages of Donnay's " Lovers " or Schnitzler's

" Liebelei "! If the love-making of the average American on the stage is strange, the other sort of sentimentalizing is none the less unaccountable. On page 329, where there should be none of the poetry and passion of youth, we find another proposal—twenty years after the first—where the lover appears to be retrospectively sentimental:

Jack.—Wouldn't it be a pretty finish if you took my hand and I could walk right up to the camera and say, " I told you so "—? You know I always felt that you were coming back.

Helen.—Oh, did you?

Jack (playfully, and going right center).—Had a candle burning in the window every night.

Helen.—You're sure it wasn't a red light?

Jack (remonstrating).—Dear Helen! have some poetry in your composition. Literally " red light," of course—but the real flame was here—(*hand on breast*)—a flickering hope that somewhere—somehow —somewhen I should be at rest—with the proud Helen that loved and—rode away.

Helen (almost accusingly).—I—believe—you.

Jack.—Of course you believe me.

4. There are many episodes, incidents, and plots begun in the first act. Study this act carefully and trace each of the important references to superstition and telepathy, each of the " love-scenes," the murder, etc., and notice how each is further developed in the play. Is the first act too crowded? What is its unity? Who is the villain?

WILLIAM GILLETTE

William Gillette was born at Hartford, Connecticut, in 1855. He was carefully educated, attended college at Yale and Harvard and the Massachusetts Fine Arts Institute. "It seems that as far back as nursery days the boy owned his miniature theater, and was quick in his mechanical inventions." His first appearance as an actor was made in 1875, and he still acts, for the most part in his own plays. His first play, "The Professor," was written in 1881.

Like many other American dramatists, Gillette is clever, amusing, technically efficient, and interesting, but not significant or illuminating. A polished and intelligent actor, he knows well the requirements of the stage, and for over thirty years he has given the public what it wanted. His Civil War plays—especially "Secret Service" and "Held by the Enemy"—are among the best American plays yet written, while "Too Much Johnson" and "Sherlock Holmes," the one a farce, the other a detective play, are justly estimated as among the best of their type this country has seen.

PLAYS

The Professor (1881).
Esmeralda (in collaboration with Mrs. Burnett, 1881).

HELD BY THE ENEMY (1886).

A LEGAL WRECK (1888).

MR. WILKINSON'S WIDOWS (1891).

NINETY DAYS (1893).

TOO MUCH JOHNSON (1894).

SECRET SERVICE (1896).

SHERLOCK HOLMES (1899).

CLARICE (1905).

THAT LITTLE AFFAIR AT BOYD'S (1908).

THE ROBBER (1909).

AMONG THIEVES (1909).

ELECTRICITY (1910).

There are, besides the above, six or eight adaptations, translations, and dramatizations, and one vaudeville sketch.

"Esmeralda," "Held by the Enemy," "Too Much Johnson," and "Secret Service" are published by Samuel French; "Electricity" in *The Drama*, Nov., 1913.

REFERENCES: Montrose J. Moses, "The American Dramatist" (Little, Brown); Richard Burton, "The New American Drama" (Crowell); Charlton Andrews, "The Drama of To-day" (Lippincott); Brander Matthews, "Study of the Drama" (Houghton Mifflin).—*Magazines: Drama*, Nov., 1913; *Bookman*, vol. xxxii (p. 594); *Everybody's*, vol. xxxi. (p. 257); *Outlook*, vol. cii (p. 947).

HELD BY THE ENEMY

A war drama in five acts. First performed in 1886.

"Held by the Enemy" is pure amusement. There is no "idea," as in "The Witching Hour," no thesis or problem; it is merely a vehicle for the telling of an exciting story of arms and a love-affair.

1. There are very few war plays which concern themselves solely with the war: nearly always there is some personal plot, usually a love-story, running through it. One of the most famous of war plays, Sardou's "Patrie!" (published in the "Drama League Series," Doubleday, Page and Co.), makes use of the war element as a dramatic background to a personal drama of love and honor; Clyde Fitch's "Nathan Hale" is treated in somewhat the same manner; likewise Gillette's "Secret Service." Is "Held by the Enemy" a war play with an element of love interest, or a love-story with a war background?

Why does Gillette start this play with a personal episode? Why not begin with the military part?

2. The influence of the actor on the drama has ever been an important consideration to the drama-

tist. In his "Study of the Drama" Professor
Matthews mentions numerous plays which either
came into existence or were modified to their present form as a result of the dramatist's collaboration with his actors. He quotes Legouvé to the
effect that "dramatists did well to study the qualities of the contemporary actors, but . . . there
was a more constant advantage in availing one's
self also of the defects of these performers—' since
their merits might abandon them, whereas their
faults would never leave them.'" In Montrose J.
Moses's "The American Dramatist" the author in
speaking of Gillette says, "But he is distinctively
unemotional. Even in simple love scenes . . . he
makes appeal through the sentiment of situation,
through the exquisite sensitiveness of outward detail, rather than through romantic attitude and
heart fervor." This may well account for the lack
of passion in the present play. Gillette has acted
in nearly all his own plays, and the principal parts
must of course be in accord with his own qualities.
Possibly when Thomas wrote "The Witching
Hour" he was well aware of the ability and shortcomings of his actors.

"Held by the Enemy" and "The Witching
Hour" must be read rather as skeletons or scena-
rios upon which the actors must elaborate, than
rounded wholes, like the plays of Shaw and
Barrie. American dramatists write with no other

idea than that of stage presentation, the English write both for the stage and the library.

3. Gillette is a disciple in the "well-made plays" school. His melodramas have sometimes been criticised for their geometrical symmetry. In what way are they symmetrical? Are they too nicely balanced? Compare them with Brieux's "The Three Daughters of M. Dupont" and Hervieu's "The Labyrinth."

4. Is there any attempt at individual characterization, or are the personages all types? Is the actor given much leeway?

5. It is interesting to compare the utterances of practising dramatists on the subject of their art. Augustus Thomas expressed himself (p. 238) as a playwright of and for the masses, and Gillette's statement differs little in essence: "We find that public honest and straightforward with us always, ever ready to be moved by what is true and lifelike and human, *provided* it be made interesting; ever ready to reject the false and artificial, even though it be festooned with literary gems."

CLYDE FITCH

Clyde Fitch was born at Elmira, New York, in 1865. He went to college at Amherst; immediately after his graduation he began writing: at first, light poems, then short stories and sketches. In 1890 he began his career as a dramatist with the romantic "Beau Brummel," written for Richard Mansfield. He continued his successful career for nearly twenty years, dying in 1909, at Châlons-sur-Marne, in France.

Fitch was a clever and ingenious writer of comedies, picturing for the most part the life of the "upper classes" in New York. His facility, his power of observation of externals, his constant application to what was curious and amusing in life rather than what was significant, added to an inherent lack of concentration, prevented his being a man of genius. His ideas on the drama have been best expressed by himself: "I feel myself very strongly the particular value—a value which, rightly or wrongly, I can't help feeling inestimable—in a modern play, of reflecting absolutely and truthfully the life and environment about us; every class, every kind, every emotion, every motive, every occupation, every business, every idleness! Never was life so varied, so complex. . . . Take what strikes you most, in the hope it will interest others; take what suits you most to do—what perhaps you can do best, and then do it better. Be truthful, and then nothing can be too big, nothing should be too small, so long as it is here and there. . . . If you inculcate an idea into your play, so much the better for your play and for you and for your audience. In fact, there is small hope for your play as a play, if you have not some idea in it, somewhere and somehow, even if it is hidden. It is sometimes better for you if it is hidden, but it must of course be integral. . . . One should write what one sees, but observe under the surface. It is a mistake to look at the reflection of the sky in the water of theatrical convention; instead, look up and into the sky of real life itself."

PLAYS

Beau Brummel (1890).

Betty's Finish (1890).

Frédéric Lemaître (1890).

A Modern Match (Marriage) (1891).

Pamela's Prodigy (1891).

The Social Swim (1893).

His Grace de Grammont (1894).

April Weather (1894).

Gossip (in collaboration with Leo Dietrichstein, 1895).

A Superfluous Husband (in collaboration with the same, 1897).

Nathan Hale (1898).

The Moth and the Flame (1898).

The Cowboy and the Lady (1899).

Barbara Frietchie (1899).

THE CLIMBERS (1900).

CAPTAIN JINKS OF THE HORSE MARINES (1901).

LOVERS' LANE (1901).

THE LAST OF THE DANDIES (1901).

THE WAY OF THE WORLD (1901).

THE GIRL AND THE JUDGE (1901).

THE STUBBORNNESS OF GERALDINE (1902).

THE GIRL WITH THE GREEN EYES (1902).

THE BIRD IN THE CAGE (1903).

HER OWN WAY (1903).

GLAD OF IT (1903).

MAJOR ANDRÉ (1903).

THE CORONET OF A DUCHESS (1904).

GRANNY (1904).

COUSIN BILLY (1904).

THE WOMAN IN THE CASE (1904).

HER GREAT MATCH (1905).

WOLFVILLE (1905).

THE GIRL WHO HAS EVERYTHING (1906).

THE TRUTH (1906).

THE STRAIGHT ROAD (1906).

HER SISTER (1907).

GIRLS (1908).

A HAPPY MARRIAGE (1909).

THE BACHELOR (1909).

THE CITY (1910).

There are, besides these, a number of adaptations and dramatizations.

"Pamela's Prodigy" is published by Allen, New York (out of print); "Nathan Hale" is published by Baker, Boston. "Barbara Frietchie," "Beau

Brummel," "The Climbers," "Captain Jinks of the
Horse Marines," "The Stubbornness of Geraldine,"
"The Girl with the Green Eyes," "Her Own Way,"
"The Truth" are published by Samuel French;
"The Truth" is also included in "Chief Contem-
porary Dramatists" (Houghton Mifflin).

REFERENCES: Montrose J. Moses, "The American
Dramatist" (Little, Brown), "Clyde Fitch: A Trib-
ute," in Fitch's "A Wave of Life" (Kennerley);
Richard Burton, "The New American Drama"
(Crowell); L. W. Strang, "Plays and Players of
the Last Quarter Century"; Charlton Andrews, "The
Drama To-day" (Lippincott); William Archer,
"Playmaking" (Small, Maynard); Brander Mat-
thews, "A Study of the Drama" (Houghton Mifflin);
Archibald Henderson, "The Changing Drama"
(Holt); Archie Bell, "The Clyde Fitch I Knew"
(Broadway Pub. Co.); Walter Prichard Eaton, "At
the New Theater, and Others" (Small, Maynard);
Arthur Ruhl, "Second Nights" (Scribner).—*Magazines: Nation,* vol. lxxxiv (p. 526); *Independent,* vol.
lxvii (p. 123); *Scribner's,* vol. lxvii (p. 490); *Theatre,*
vol. vii (p. 14); *Putnam's,* vol. vii (p. 244); *Harper's
Weekly,* vol. xlvi (p. 20); *Book Buyer,* vol. xvii (p.
118), vol. xvi (p. 323); *Current Literature,* vol. xlvii
(p. 552), vol. xlvii (p. 362); *Bookman,* vol. xxx (p.
135), vol. xxiii (p. 63); *Literary Digest,* vol. xxxix
(p. 171), vol. xxxiv (p. 437); *Dramatic Mirror,* Sept.
18, 1909; *Forum,* vol. xlv (p. 221); *Critic,* vol. xxxviii
(p. 225).

(During the present year, 1915, Little, Brown and

Co. are to publish a Memorial Edition of Fitch's plays. Three plays, hitherto unpublished, will be added: " The City," " Lovers' Lane," and " The Woman in the Case." There will be critical and historical .material by Montrose J. Moses and by Fitch himself.)

THE TRUTH

A play in four acts. First performed in 1906.

"The Truth" is probably Clyde Fitch's most consistent and best-sustained play. There is in it less of the amusingly irrelevant, and more study and observation of character than in even "The Girl with the Green Eyes" or "The Climbers." The universality of theme, unity, and sincerity, is evidenced by the fact that the play has been successfully produced in England and in many countries of the Continent. Usually, Fitch was wont to rely on his instinct and upon some novel device independent of the integral action of the play—like the scene in the Vatican in "The Girl with the Green Eyes" or on the deck of the steamer in "The Stubbornness of Geraldine"—but in "The Truth" there is a conscious discarding of the non-essential.

1. Fitch's sense for externals is manifested on page 4:

Mrs. Lindon.—. . . Becky! One of my oldest friends! One of my bridesmaids!
Maura.—What!
Mrs. Lindon.—No, she wasn't, but she might have been; she was my next choice if any one had backed out.

253

This is amusing, and it tells something of one character—the speaker. It is a *mot de caractère*. Still, it tells nothing very deep or very significant. Later on, Mrs. Lindon's character is developed, but there is nothing very startling or new that we learn of her. In the first act is there any distinct or notable bit of information given as to any of the characters? What of Becky herself?

As the play progresses, notice by what means the character of Becky is built up. Is it through situations, by dialogue, or through the conversation of others?

2. The lie has ever been a fruitful source of dramatic material: Ibsen has dramatized it in most of his social dramas; Henry Arthur Jones—in " The Liars " and " The Lie," and Maurice Donnay in " The Free Woman "—have written effective pieces around men and women who lie to attain certain ends, and fail. Has this play of Fitch's points in common as to treatment with any of the plays here referred to? What is the dramatic, the " theatrical," essence of " The Truth "? How has the author extracted what is most interesting and appealing from his theme?

Fitch's words (quoted on pp. 248-49 of the present volume) regarding underlying ideas in plays are peculiarly apt: " If you inculcate an idea into your play so much the better for your play and for you and for your audience. . . . It is sometimes better for you if it is hidden, but it must of course be integral . . ." Is Fitch's idea hidden? Is it integral?

3. The American habit of bringing a play to a happy ending is a result of the intellectual youth of the country. The average audience has not yet come to the point where it will unflinchingly accept the logical consequences of a situation. Eugene Walter in " The Easiest Way " has dared to draw his tragic play to its ruthless and only possible close, but he succeeded only in spite of this fact, by reason of deft craftsmanship. No one objects to the happy ending of a happy play; the fault lies with the dramatist who begins with a situation and characters from which only evil or tragedy can come. Bernard Veiller's " Within the Law," George Broadhurst's " Bought and Paid For," both began with interesting and serious problems, but each dramatist, either because he was incapable of sustained thinking and reasoning power —which is unlikely—escaped from his main theme, and allowed his play to drift on the current of amusing but utterly inconsequential circumstances.

If a dramatist introduces a certain character early in the play with the idea of changing the mind and spirit of that character, he must motivate each action and account for the character at the end of the play. If Ibsen wished to show Nora as a doll in the first act of " A Doll's House," and a mature and thinking woman in the last, he must adduce convincing proofs of the metamorphosis. Henry Arthur Jones, in " The Crusaders " and " Dolly Reforming Herself," ridicules the attempts of would-be reformers to accomplish their ends over-night, as it were: the " crusaders," in the one, and Dolly and her friends in the other, are sadder and wiser at last, but they are no nearer to reformation than when the curtain first rose. In Hermann Bahr's " Das Konzert " the philandering artist will, we are positive, continue to give " concerts " as long as he is so inclined; in Leo Dietrichstein's American version, called " The Concert," the amiable pianist assures his wife that he will " give no more concerts." Very often a dramatist will throw a sop to his exigent audience, but at the same time add a " tag " showing that the " lived happily ever after " is but the merest convention. Hubert Henry Davies' " The Mollusc " is a case in question: Tom's words, which close the play, are: " Were those miracles permanent cures? (*Shakes his head.*) We're never told! We're never told!" This is legitimate, like the happy ending to a fairy-story, but when the inexorable logic of life demands truth, and the dramatist deliberately distorts the truth, the play is false.

Study carefully the last act of " The Truth," determining exactly how genuine is Becky's " conversion," whether the author intended his audience to accept the *dénouement*, or whether he intended the closing lines to put the audience in a good humor. Notice, however, the extreme cleverness of the end:

Becky.—You can't forgive me!

Warder.—We don't love people because they are perfect.

(*He takes her two trembling hands in his, and she rises.*)

Becky.—Tom!

Warder.—We love them because they are themselves.

WILLIAM VAUGHN MOODY

William Vaughn Moody was born at Spencer, Indiana, in 1869. He was educated at Harvard. For some years he wrote poems and poetic dramas, while he filled the position of professor of English at the University of Chicago. "The Great Divide"—originally "A Sabine Woman"—was produced in 1906. "The Faith Healer," a failure, was produced three years later. Moody died in 1910.

Moody is a man of one play, yet so full of promise was "The Great Divide," so American in the best sense, that his early death cannot but be the source of the deepest regret. He had within him the instinct of the dramatist, together with the conscience and taste of an artist. The poet in him felt the romance and beauty of the East and West in America, and he combined felicity of language with stirring incidents and an interesting if questionable problem. In "The Faith Healer" he was led astray by an idea; still, the play was an advance in so far as it showed greater unity and a firmer grasp of his idea than did "The Great Divide." Moody took American drama where Thomas left it, and pointed a way at least to what possibilities lay beyond.

PLAYS

The Great Divide (1906).
The Faith Healer (1909).

Both these are published in "Poems and Plays of William Vaughn Moody," Vol. II (Houghton Mifflin). "The Great Divide" is included in "Chief Contemporary Dramatists" (Houghton Mifflin).

REFERENCES: Montrose J. Moses, "The American Dramatist" (Little, Brown); Richard Burton, "The New American Drama" (Crowell); Charlton Andrews, "The Drama To-day" (Lippincott); William Archer, "Playmaking" (Small, Maynard); Archibald Henderson, "The Changing Drama" (Holt); Arthur Ruhl, "Second Nights" (Scribner); Frank Wadleigh Chandler, "Aspects of Modern Drama" (Macmillan); "Some Letters of William Vaughn Moody" (Houghton Mifflin); Edwin Herbert Lewis, "William Vaughn Moody" (Chicago Literary Club); J. M. Manly, Introduction to collected Houghton Mifflin edition.—*Magazines: Drama,* May, 1911; *Dial,* vol. xlvii (p. 330), vol. liii (p. 484); *Nation,* vol. xci (p. 352); *Independent,* vol. lxxiv (p. 314); *University of Chicago Magazine,* vol. v (p. 152); *Yale Review,* vol. ii (p. 688); *Bookman,* vol. xxxii (p. 249).

THE GREAT DIVIDE

A play in three acts. First performed in 1906.

" The Great Divide " is a psychological character-study with a Western background during part of the action, and its very antithesis—New England—for the rest. Its value as an acting play is attested by the fact that for at least two years it enjoyed great success in the large cities and on the road, and is still a stock favorite.

1. As in " King Lear," the first act of this play contains a climactic scene, after which there is a decided fall, a relaxing of dramatic tension, and an explanation. The case comes first, then the discussion and the problem. In Shakspere's play the action rises again to a still higher pitch of tension ; is this so in " The Great Divide "? William Archer, in " Playmaking," criticises the play because, " after the stirring first act," it " is weakened by our sense that the happy ending is only being postponed by a violent effort. We have been assured from the very first—even before Ruth Jordan has set eyes on Stephen Ghent—that just such a rough diamond is the ideal of her dreams . . . the author has taken such pains to emphasize the fact that these two people are really made for each

other, that the answer to the question is not for a moment in doubt, and we become rather impatient of the obstinate sulkiness of Ruth's attitude." The criticism is just enough, but there is a graver one: not only is the audience impatient as to the psychological development, but the action drags. How could the dramatist have remedied the defect?

2. It is natural that the prose work of a poet should bear some impress of his feeling for the beauty of language. The style of this play is on the whole *literary* in the dramatic sense: that is, it is in accordance with the character of the speakers. Into the mouth of the refined Ruth the dramatist has legitimately put many beautiful speeches, but as these are revelatory of her mind and temperament they are not out of place. This sense of literary effect has been admirably combined with the purely theatrical in the first act (pp. 290-91, " Chief Contemporary Dramatists ") :

What a lovely night! Who would ever think to call this a desert, this moonlit ocean of flowers? What millions of cactus blooms have opened since yesterday!

And later on; after she sings the three verses of the song:

Be still, you beauties! You'll drive me to distraction with your color and your odor. I'll take a hostage for your good behavior.

(*She selects a red flower, puts it in the dark mass of her hair, and looks out at the open door.*)

What a scandal the moon is making, out there in that great crazy world! Who but me could think of sleeping on such a night?

(*She sits down, folds the flowers in her arms, and buries her face in them.*)

Add to this the effective contrast of the following scene, and there can remain no doubt that this is the work of a man of the theater.

3. After such an act there could come only an anti-climax; the explanation and development following the big scene would probably have been much more interesting had it not been for the graphic and exciting first act. How does the author seek to arouse interest and create suspense again? Is the end of the second act sufficiently tense to force the audience to await impatiently the rise of the curtain on the final act? What of the last act itself? Is the happy ending logical? Compare it with the endings of " Young Mrs. Winthrop " and " The Witching Hour."

PERCY MACKAYE

Percy Mackaye was born at New York City, in 1875. He is the son of Steele Mackaye, author of " Hazel Kirke." He graduated from Harvard, where he was a student under Professor Baker. A poet of taste and feeling, he has written a number of poetic dramas, a few prose comedies and fantasies, most of which have been produced, though none with any considerable degree of commercial success.

Mackaye possesses what most American dramatists lack: a definite ideal. He lacks what Thomas and Fitch and Gillette have to a marked degree: a sense of the theater. He writes well, too well in places, for his dialogue is often " literary "; his sense of construction is occasionally faulty, and many of his plays tend to drag. Still, his influence is beneficial, his ideals are sure to bear fruit, and he may yet write what he has twice come near to writing: a true American comedy. " Jeanne D'Arc " and " Sapho and Phaon " are good closet dramas, " Mater " is a delightful prose satire, " Anti-Matrimony " delicate high-farce, and " The Scarecrow " nearly a masterpiece of imaginative writing, while " A Thousand Years Ago "—an Oriental fantasy—is as delightful as anything of its kind written in recent years. Mackaye is also a lecturer and writer on matters pertaining to the stage.

PLAYS

THE CANTERBURY PILGRIMS (1903).
JEANNE D'ARC (1906).
FENRIS THE WOLF (1905).
SAPHO AND PHAON (1908).
MATER (1910).
THE SCARECROW (1910).
ANTI-MATRIMONY (1910).
YANKEE FANTASIES (one-act plays) (1911).
TO-MORROW (1913).
A THOUSAND YEARS AGO (1914).

("The Canterbury Pilgrims" was not produced until 1909; "Fenris the Wolf" and "To-morrow" have not yet been professionally produced; some of the "Yankee Fantasies" have been privately produced. The dates of these plays refer to publication.)

"Jeanne D'Arc," "Fenris the Wolf," "Sapho and Phaon," "Mater," "The Canterbury Pilgrims," and "The Scarecrow" are published by Macmillan; "Yankee Fantasies" by Duffield; "Anti-Matrimony" and "To-morrow" by Stokes; and "A Thousand Years Ago" in the "Drama League Series" by Doubleday, Page. "The Scarecrow" is included in "Chief Contemporary Dramatists" (Houghton Mifflin).

REFERENCES: Montrose J. Moses, "The American Dramatist" (Little, Brown); Richard Burton, "The New American Drama" (Crowell); Brander Matthews, "A Study of the Drama" (Houghton Mifflin); Charles Wadleigh Chandler, "Aspects of

Modern Drama " (Macmillan); Charlton Andrews,
" The Drama To-day " (Lippincott); Percy Mackaye,
" The Playhouse and the Play " (Macmillan), and
" The Civic Theater " (Kennerley).—*Magazines:*
Outlook, vol. lxxxv (p. 302), vol. cii (p. 953); *North
American,* vol. clxxxviii (p. 404); *Current Literature,*
vol. xlv (p. 554); *Scribner's,* vol. xlvi (p. 28); *Book-
man,* vol. xxxii (p. 249), vol. xxxvi (p. 12).

THE SCARECROW

"A tragedy of the ludicrous." A play in four acts.
First performed in 1910.

"The Scarecrow" is founded upon Hawthorne's
story of "Feathertop." The play is by no means a
dramatization, but an independent work of which only
the skeleton was taken from Hawthorne. Percy Mackaye's ideas, his literary sense, his dramatic feeling,
are nowhere so much in evidence as in "The Scarecrow": here is effective drama—no one who saw the
production in 1910 can doubt it—an interesting theme,
well worked out, and skilful handling of such externals as will attract and hold.

1. Mackaye was wise in making as direct and
visible an appeal as possible in his first act: the
mysterious blacksmith shop, the "horned and
tailed" devil, the suggestion of witchcraft, all tend
to create an atmosphere proper for the unfolding
of the plot and exposition of ideas. The poet does
not actually begin his play until the external appeal has been definitely made.

What dramatic, as distinct from literary, ex-
pedients are used in this first act to accomplish
the ends just mentioned?

2. The idea of the play is not at first easy to define: there is first the " mirror of truth " episode, then the Justice Merton and Goody Rickby story, and so on. These finally mould themselves into an harmonious whole, which eventually yields the theme of the play. But each individual thread of action is developed in a leisurely manner. In the second act, for example, there is none of the usual American haste—no " punch," no purely theatrical situations: the poet has found a suitable vehicle for drama as well as for poetic prose. Does he ever allow his theme or his liking for the purely literary to interfere with the dramatic development of the story? If so, where?

3. The climax at the end of the third act is according to the formulas of the well-made play: in its proper place. From the somewhat loose beginning of the second act, trace the process whereby the dramatist has brought his unusual play to a usual climactic point. Does he eliminate or relegate to the background threads of interest which are not so important as the main one—as Jones does in " The Liars "—or does he temporarily thrust the important ones into the foreground, asking the audience to accept it for the time being?

4. Consider the last act in the light of its effectiveness as a stage play; is there too much theme, and insufficient action?

Why does Ravensbane die at the end? The last two speeches are:

Richard (bending over him).—Dead!
Rachel (with an exalted look).—But a man!

Is this the " Tragedy of the Ludicrous "?

EDWARD SHELDON

Edward Sheldon was born at Chicago in 1886. He attended college at Harvard, where he was a member of Professor Baker's class in dramatic technic, and was graduated in 1907. After the production of his first play, " Salvation Nell," by Mrs. Fiske, his success was assured.

Sheldon is a brilliant and talented young man with true dramatic instinct. His first play, " Salvation Nell," is notable by reason of its minute observation of externals; " The Nigger," because of its theme, came near to being a significant play; " The Boss " and " The High Road " are less interesting pictures of various phases of contemporaneous American life; while " Romance," as a story pure and simple, is one of the best-made plays of the day. Sheldon is enterprising, and in each of his plays he experiments with form. He has a constant tendency toward the melodramatic, the conventional and the sentimental, but his solider gifts afford promise of something truly large and typically American.

PLAYS

Salvation Nell (1908).
The Nigger (1909).
The Boss (1911).
Princess Zim-Zam (1911).

EGYPT (1912).

THE HIGH ROAD (1912).

ROMANCE (1913).

THE SONG OF SONGS (based upon the novel of Hermann Sudermann, 1914).

THE GARDEN OF PARADISE (1915).

" The Nigger," " Romance," and " The Garden of Paradise " are published separately by Macmillan.

REFERENCES: Montrose J. Moses, " The American Dramatist" (Little, Brown); Richard Burton, " The New American Drama " (Crowell); Frank Wadleigh Chandler, " Aspects of Modern Drama " (Macmillan); William Archer, " Playmaking" (Small, Maynard); Clayton Hamilton, " Studies in Stagecraft" (Holt); Walter Prichard Eaton, " At the New Theater, and Others " (Small, Maynard); Charlton Andrews, " The Drama To-day " (Lippincott).—*Magazines: Current Opinion,* vol. liv (p. 379); *Outlook,* vol. cii (p. 947); *Bookman,* vol. xxx (p. 463), vol. xxxvii (p. 306), vol. xl (p. 637); *New Republic,* vol. i (p. 23).

ROMANCE

A play in three acts, a prologue, and an epilogue.
First performed in 1913.

"Romance" is the most close-knit and logical of
this dramatist's plays. While the subject-matter is not
distinctively American, the details, the development,
and the point of view are indubitably so.

1. From time to time, and of recent years especially, a dramatist has set a play within a play,
or in some other manner arranged the time-scheme
of his play, in order to achieve some novelty of
effect. "Milestones" by Bennett and Knoblauch
has three acts, the first of which takes place in
the sixties, the second in the eighties, and the last
in the year 1912. Sheldon's "The High Road"
is in five acts, which cover a period of about twenty-
five years; George Cohan's dramatization of "The
Seven Keys to Baldpate" is a play within a play;
"The Big Idea," by A. E. Thomas and Clayton
Hamilton, is still another novelty in stagecraft;
while "On Trial," by Elmer Reizenstein, tells a
story in reverse chronological order.

The value of this transposition of the time-
scheme usually lies in the novelty, but—and this

is especially true in the case of " On Trial "—the
novelty soon wears off. There a commonplace
melodramatic incident is made interesting only because it is told in the reverse order; the pleasure
is felt only in seeing *how* it is done. Like a
clever acrobatic feat, once it is over there is no
desire to see it repeated. Where the device is not
so novel and involved, as in " Milestones," or where
it is more legitimately used, as in the plays of
Cohan, A. E. Thomas, and Clayton Hamilton, more
attention can be paid to the play itself. But as a
matter of fact the unfolding of the past has been
much more skilfully and naturally accomplished in
many of the plays of Ibsen, and especially in Hjal-
mar Bergström's powerful play, " Karen Borneman." " Ghosts " and " Rosmersholm " accomplish practically the same ends as does " On Trial,"
only there is no *visible* return to the past: it is unfolded by means of dialogue and its results are made
manifest in the present. " On Trial " interests
us only when the past is visibly returned to, with
the result that it is made too vivid, and the proper
perspective lost. The past cannot be so vivid as
the present. In " Karen Borneman " the past rises
up gradually; in fact, there is a great deal of
exposition in the last act, but as the facts are
made known as they would be in life itself, as a
result of certain other facts, the audience keeps
pace with the characters, and is never " ahead of

the game." The only criticism to be made against such plays as " On Trial " is that their very novelty is soon outworn, and that it is above all useless.

" Romance " is the visualization of a story of the past. But as that story is the play, the prologue may be taken as incidental: as a frame for the principal action. However, had the story in the prologue been made more important, the intrusion of the old man's story would have thrown into exaggerated relief what should have been only a detail.

2. It has already been remarked that one of the vices of American drama is its sentimentality, and Edward Sheldon has not yet been able to escape it. Needless to say the very title of the play implies sentiment, and its theme demands vigorous treatment. Yet, on the stage or off, sentiment is sentiment, and any exaggeration is false. In the third act we find the following speech of Tom:

. . . Don't you hear the midnight cry: " Behold The Bridegroom cometh. Go ye out to meet Him! " Don't you see Him coming from the wilderness like a pillar of smoke, perfumed with myrrh and frankincense? His eyes are as a flame of fire, and on His head are many crowns. He wears a garment dipped in blood and on it a name is written, Lord of Lords and King of Kings! Hark! He is outside knocking at

your door! Rose of Sharon, Lily of the Valley, cease
your slumber, for the hour has come!

These words, to be sure, are put into the mouth
of the passionate young rector, but it is a question
whether the author was not striving to attain an
effect independent of what the logic of the situation required. In "The High Road" he attempted this, to the detriment of the truth of the
situation.

Sheldon has always been lavish in the use of
crowds, brass bands, and the like. These are of
course always effective, but their constant use
tends to weaken the effect of the play. At the
end of "The Nigger," in the big act of "The
Boss," and at the end of "The High Road,"
there are "mobs outside"; what of these devices
in "Romance"? The touch of melodrama which
often nearly spoils an otherwise dramatic scene
is painfully evident in the last act of the present
play:

(*Pause. They are both breathing deeply. Tom,
biting his underlip and never taking his eyes off her
face, is crawling softly up on her other side, crouched
like a beast prepared to spring upon her unaware.
Then, in the silence, just as he is ready to leap, is
heard the first note of the midnight bell. The full,
deep tones strike solemnly and slowly up to twelve.
Then, as it continues, the sound of a choir of men's*

voices, sturdy and sweet, is heard from far away,
gradually growing nearer. They are playing and sing-
ing the old Lutheran hymn " Ein' feste Burg." As
Tom hears them, he gradually straightens and his old
look and manner come back to him. He goes rather
unsteadily. He stands for a moment looking out; then
turns to Rita, passing his hand over his forehead as
one recovering from a dream.)

Add to this the phonograph playing Caval-
lini's song!

3. Sheldon is rarely mistaken as to the effect
he wishes to produce, and his plays are full of
minor points which are admirably done: the quaint
incident in " The Boss " where the principal character buys the brooch and examines it; the scene
in the Governor's office in " The High Road ";
most of the first act of " Salvation Nell," are
peculiarly Sheldonian. These touches go far to
create charm and build up character. What examples are there in " Romance "? How far is
the dramatist dependent upon them for the creation of his larger effects?

EUGENE WALTER

Eugene Walter was born in 1876. He did reporting on a Cleveland newspaper, then joined the New York *Sun,* and served in the army. For some years he was advance agent for a number of theatrical companies. For the past eight or nine years he has devoted himself exclusively to the writing of plays.

Walter is a born man of the theater. His plays are for the most part melodramatic situations à la Bernstein, well developed, skilfully constructed, employing an American background as a matter of course. He is little concerned with ideas or characterization. He is journalistic, violent, and nearly always interesting. His violence leads him at times to excesses, but it sometimes drives him relentlessly into powerful and gripping situations. " Paid in Full " and " The Easiest Way," in particular, are fearless in their logic, and the author has fortunately not given in to the temptation to do violence to the logic of situation and character by making happy endings. " Fine Feathers " is uneven, but contains in the last two acts many scenes of high merit. Walter makes no pretension to " uplifting " the drama, he possesses no literary sense, his ideal is solely that of supplying the stage with dramatic stories.

PLAYS

The Undertow (1907).
Sergeant James (1907).
Paid in Full (1907).
The Wolf (1908).
The Easiest Way (1908).
Just a Wife (1910).
Boots and Saddles (from "Sergeant James," 1910).
The Trail of the Lonesome Pine (1911).
Fine Feathers (1912).

None of the above has been published in play form, although " The Easiest Way " has been " novelized " (by A. Hornblow; G. W. Dillingham, publisher).

(Note: Walter is another dramatist, like Herne and Cohan and Klein, whose plays, not being obtainable, cannot be studied in connection with the present outline. The novelization, however, contains practically all the dialogue, and the play itself is in some of the larger public libraries.)

References: Montrose J. Moses, " The American Dramatist " (Little, Brown); Richard Burton, " The New American Drama " (Crowell); Charlton Andrews, " The Drama To-day " (Lippincott); Archibald Henderson, " The Changing Drama " (Holt).— *Magazines: Harper's Weekly,* vol. lii (p. 28); *Current Literature,* vol. liii (p. 443); *Bookman,* vol. xxxii (p. 294).

THE EASIEST WAY

A play in four acts. First performed in 1908.

A comparison of " The Easiest Way " with Pinero's
" Iris " immediately suggests itself, and a good deal
might be said on the subject. However, whether Walter was acquainted with the English play or not, he
has treated a similar theme in a rather dissimilar manner. Pinero's story is occasionally subtle, always ingenious; Walter's is direct, brutal, though undoubtedly
stronger. Pinero's woman is universal and possibly
lacking therefore in recognizably familiar touches.
Walter's is definitely " human," particular, American.

The style of dialogue in " Iris " is rarely collo-
quial; that in " The Easiest Way " is almost too
much so. On page 9 (of the private edition of
the play) Will says:

Yes, it's been a mighty good two years for me.
I was always proud to take you around, because I
think you one of the prettiest things in New York
(*Laura crosses R., and girlishly jumps into armchair*),
and that helps some, and you're always jolly, and
you never complained. You always spent a lot of
money, but it was a pleasure to see you spend it; and
then you never offended me. Most women offend men

by coming around untidy and sort of unkempt, but
somehow you always knew the value of your beauty,
and you always dressed up. I always thought that
maybe some day the fellow would come along, grab
you, and make you happy in a nice way, but I thought
that he'd have to have a lot of money. You know
you've lived a rather extravagant life for five years,
Laura. It won't be an easy job to come down to cases
and suffer for the little dainty necessities you've been
used to.

An interesting contrast is afforded in a comparison of the endings of the two plays (see p. 22,
present volume). Walter ends his play as follows:

Laura (*suddenly arousing herself, and with a de-
fiant voice*).—No, I'm not. I'm going to stay right
here. (*Annie crosses and opens trunk L., takes out
handsome dress, crosses, hangs it over back of armchair R. C., crosses up to hat trunk, takes out hat.
Laura takes it from her, crosses to trunk L., starts to
unpack it.*) Open these trunks, take out those clothes,
get me my prettiest dress. Hurry up. (*She goes before the mirror.*) Get my new hat, dress up my body,
and paint up my face. It 's all they've left of me.
(*To herself.*) They've taken my soul away with
them.

Annie (*in a happy voice*).—Yassum, yassum.

Laura (*who is arranging her hair*).—Doll me up,
Annie.

Annie.—Yuh goin' out, Miss Laura?

Laura.—Yes. I'm going to Rector's to make a hit, and to hell with the rest.

(*At this moment the hurdy-gurdy in the street, presumably immediately under her window, begins to play the tune of "Bon-Bon Buddie, My Chocolate Drop." There is something in this rag-time melody which is particularly and peculiarly suggestive of the low life, the criminality and prostitution that constitute the night excitement of that section of New York City known as the Tenderloin. The tune, its association, is like spreading before Laura's eyes a panorama of the inevitable depravity that awaits her. She is torn from every ideal that she so weakly endeavored to grasp, and is thrown into the mire and slime at the very moment when her emancipation seems to be assured. The woman with her flashy dress in one arm and her equally exaggerated type of picture hat in the other, is nearly prostrated by the tune and the realization of the future as it is terrifically conveyed to her. The negress, in the happiness of serving Laura in her questionable career, picks up the melody and hums it as she unpacks the finery that has been put away in the trunk.*)

Laura (*with infinite grief, resignation, and hopelessness*).—O God—O my God. (*She turns and totters toward the bedroom. The hurdy-gurdy continues, with the negress accompanying it.*)

A slow curtain.

NOTES

The theatrical situation in America is a peculiar one: many of the most successful dramatists refuse to publish their plays in book form, and a number of those who under a less rigid system of managerial policy would have ample opportunity of seeing their plays produced have been forced to resort to publication of plays which are by reason of their subject-matter, or because of some external and practical reason, kept from the professional stage. While the author has consistently held to the belief that the play which cannot be acted is not a play, and that the " closet-drama " is a form apart, he still believes that owing to local conditions certain plays which have not received the sanction of stage-presentation are legitimate examples of American tendencies. The following pages contain a few suggestions for the study of certain plays of the sort referred to, as well as further brief outlines for three or four dramatists of the other kind: those who will not allow their plays to be published.

GEORGE MIDDLETON

George Middleton is an earnest idealist, who has published three volumes of one-act plays and

one three-act comedy.* In his introduction to
"Possession," his latest volume, he says: "The
dramatist . . . who prefers to follow the impulse within him, irrespective of whether or not his
play may have a wide popular appeal, has had little
encouragement. This is obviously so where his
subjects are quietly intimate and where the clash
of character is subtly mental or emotional; especially when one compares such plays with those
others, no more dramatic in essence, which naturally command a greater audience because the
action is physical, external, and more readily com-
prehended."

Middleton, whose technical skill is seen in
his dramatizations—"The House of a Thousand
Candles" and "Barriers Burned Away"—as well
as in his own plays, has tried to make the one-act
play a vehicle for the ideas which underlie the
great movements of the day. For the most part he
has chosen to depict various aspects of the feminist
question, and his outspoken thoughts always demand thoughtful consideration. Middleton may
be criticised on the score of occasional conventionality in the matter of dialogue and perhaps a too
earnest attitude toward his "message." "I am
using," Middleton once said in an interview, "my
little one-act plays to suggest the larger drama in

* "Embers," "Tradition," "Possession," and "Nowadays" are all published by Holt.

the background. I want each play to picture either some vital past experience or some inevitable possibility which may arise. I seldom deal in finalities, since no situation in life is without its further potentialities." Here is Middleton the idealist. In two of his short plays his method may be studied: " Tradition " (in the volume under that name) and " The Groove " (in " Possession "); the first is the depiction of one aspect of a world-old struggle between radicalism and conservatism; the second is one of this dramatist's truest bits of characterization. Here is one of his best plays: it shows distinct possibilities, which should be developed and incorporated into a long play. " Nowadays," a comedy in three acts, suffers as most thesis plays do, from an overdose of thesis, but again the author's sincerity, his idealism, his sense of dramatic construction, redeem it from the realm of the purely didactic.

JOSEPHINE PRESTON PEABODY

Josephine Preston Peabody (Mrs. Marks) has achieved success with her poetic play, " The Piper," * which was produced by Winthrop Ames at the New Theater in New York. Miss Peabody

---

* Author also of " Marlowe " (1901), " The Wings " (1905), and " The Wolf of Gubbio " (1914), all published by Houghton Mifflin.

is a poetess of charm and strength, but her plays, with the single exception of " The Piper," are more effective when read than seen. If the theater and the audience had given more encouragement to writers of poetic drama, it is likely that Miss Peabody would have written more plays and less lyrics.

OLIVE TILFORD DARGAN

Olive Tilford Dargan possesses poetic gifts and some knowledge of stage requirements. " The Shepherd " and " The Mortal Gods " might, with skilful and sympathetic stage-management, prove dramatic on the stage.

HARRY BENRIMO AND GEORGE C. HAZELTON

" The Yellow Jacket " * is one of the most charming and original of modern American plays. Its charm and originality, however, militated against it as a popular success, although it called forth unstinted praise from nearly all the critics of the country.

PERCY MACKAYE

Percy Mackaye has written closet dramas as well as acting plays: " Saint Louis, a Masque." " Sanctuary, a Bird Masque," " A Garland for

* Published by Bobbs-Merrill.

Sylvia," "Fenris the Wolf," and "Sapho and Phaon" are written rather to be read than to be acted.

———

Some of the following dramatists would have separate chapters devoted to them, were their plays available, but so long as they are withheld, a brief summary must for the present suffice:

DAVID BELASCO

Probably the most prominent figure in the theatrical world of the past quarter-century, both as a dramatist and producer, is David Belasco.* As a dramatist, he should be considered rather as a skilful and occasionally inspired collaborator; as a producer, a careful, painstaking, and yet illuminating artist. He was the first in this country who studied stage-effects down to the minutest detail; so closely has he applied himself to this end that he has outstripped himself and become so engrossed in external effects that he has lost sight of general values. A "Belasco set" is ordinarily praised for its marvelous arrangement of *minutiæ*—the first act of "The Return of Peter Grimm" is the classic example—and credit should be given where it is due: this producer is a master of illusion. However, illusion is often substituted in his

* "May Blossom" (Samuel French) is his only published play.

productions to the detriment of the play. Often this is fortunate, for many of the plays Belasco has produced have little else to recommend them but the setting. One of the sensations of " The Governor's Lady " was the exact reproduction of a " Childs' " restaurant! One might as well go to see " The Garden of Allah " because of the *real* sand and the *real* camels! The genius of the man is seen in one act from " The Darling of the Gods," where the suggestion of unseen action in the thick of a bamboo jungle is legitimately thrilling. Belasco's plays—or rather those in which he has worked over the ideas of others—are on the whole melodramatic and sentimental: he is a past master in the art of creating a thrill. The long-lost child, death-bed scenes, the deserted sweetheart, the mysterious drop of blood, soft music, are a few among the many effects which he has on tap, so to speak. " Zaza," " The Heart of Maryland," " Madame Butterfly," " Du Barry," " The Girl of the Golden West," collaborations and adaptations, at once call up images of effective mounting, and compelling if at times exaggerated dramatic stories.

GEORGE ADE

George Ade, who suddenly sprang into fame in the early years of this century with his comic operas and his plays, is now seldom heard of. It

appears that this brilliant and amusing young
dramatist has either decided to abandon the stage
and apply himself to work of another nature, as
he once declared he would, or that he has written
himself out. "The College Widow," "The
County Chairman," and "Father and the Boys"
are genuine if eccentric and exaggerated comedies
of American life in which types are created, in the
author's words, "in such a manner as to increase
our self-respect and to give us a new insight into
our characteristics as a people."

GEORGE M. COHAN

George M. Cohan, actor, manager, composer,
and playwright, is essentially typical of Broadway
and the Broadway spirit in America. His musical
comedies, his farces, and his own acting belong to
what Walter Prichard Eaton termed the "comedy
of bad manners"; they are ingenious, always
amusing, often exaggerated, pictures of American
city life. Cohan can draw types, invent capital
situations, but he has yet to prove that he can
construct a full-length play which shall interest
and amuse from beginning to end. He is a dramatist of externals. Yet withal, he is a figure of
prominence, for he reflects an important side of
the American nature.

GEORGE H. BROADHURST

George H. Broadhurst is a popular playwright who has utilized the business and political elements in our daily life. Like Charles Klein, he uses the great political and business motifs only for background, as if he were afraid or unable to cope with problems of so momentous a nature. "The Man of the Hour" is an amusing melodrama; "Why Smith Left Home" * and "What Happened to Jones" * are amusing farces. "Bought and Paid For" had immense dramatic possibilities, but again the playwright avoided the issue.

WILLIAM C. DE MILLE

William C. De Mille, with "The Warrens of Virginia," "Strongheart," * and "The Woman," shows himself a follower of Belasco. He has an innate sense of the theater, he can write effective and moving melodrama, but like most of his fellow-workers, he makes use of business, politics—true American subjects—only as background. "The Woman," however, deserves especial notice as a well-constructed drama, consistently thought out and well written.

* Published by Samuel French.—DeMille's "Food" and "In 1999" are also published by French.

JOSEPH MEDILL PATTERSON

" Rebellion " comes as near to being an American play of ideas as any of the day, but either through lack of experience or, what is more probable, judgment, the play somehow missed fire. Like the same author's " The Fourth Estate," it is earnest and sincere, though there is in it a regrettable tendency toward the melodramatic.

LANGDON MITCHELL

" The New York Idea " * is a conventional but witty and clever comedy of manners, one of the few which this country has produced. Mitchell is practically the only dramatist (with the exception of Fitch) who is able and willing to satirize " high society " in America. " The New Marriage " (written for Mrs. Fiske, as were " The New York Idea " and " Becky Sharp ") was good as to idea, but fell far short of being a unified and interesting comedy.

CHARLES KLEIN

" The Lion and the Mouse " is among the first of the more recent American plays to utilize the theme of " high finance," the investigations into which were at the time causing widespread unrest.

* Published by Walter Baker (Boston).

While the play is marred by a distortion of facts and ideas, it is, none the less, an earnest attempt. It is to be regretted that in his other plays Charles Klein used such pertinent and interesting themes as police-court justice and the evils of metropolitan life and that in the department store, only as background. " The Third Degree," " The Gamblers," and " Maggie Pepper " fall far short of their infinite possibilities. Lately Charles Klein went to live in England; when he left he said that the American dramatist must get away from his own country in order to gain a better perspective. It is hoped that Klein will, as he can do, take his art a little more seriously, and make use of his undoubted gifts in a play which shall be workmanlike and significantly American.

RACHEL CROTHERS

" A Man's World " * is an attractive and touching picture of New York life. Miss Crothers has done notable work in this play and in " The Three of Us," " The Herfords," and " Myself, Bettina." Like other woman dramatists in America (Margaret Mayo, Eleanor Gates, Mary Roberts Rinehart, and Alice Brown), there is a certain conventionality both in the treatment of the theme and in

* Published by Badger, in the " American Dramatists' Series."

the development of human character, but a note of sincerity and a certain fidelity to external details allow one to hope that this dramatist will make further use of her talents.

BIBLIOGRAPHY

General Reference Works on the Drama, its Theory, Technic, and History:

ANDREWS, CHARLTON.
The Drama To-day. Lippincott.

ARCHER, WILLIAM.
Playmaking, a Manual of Craftsmanship. Small, Maynard.

BAKER, GEORGE P.
The Technique of the Drama. Houghton Mifflin.

BURTON, RICHARD.
How to See a Play. Macmillan.

CAFFIN, CHARLES H.
The Appreciation of the Drama. Doubleday, Page.

CANNAN, GILBERT.
The Joy of the Theater. Dutton.

CARTER, HUNTLY.
The New Spirit in Drama and Art. Kennerley.

CHANDLER, FRANK WADLEIGH.
Aspects of Modern Drama. Macmillan.
The Contemporary Drama of France. Little, Brown.

CHENEY, SHELDON.
The New Movement in the Theater. Kennerley.

CLARK, BARRETT H.
The Continental Drama of To-day. Holt.
European Theories of the Drama. Stewart &
Kidd.
Contemporary French Dramatists. Stewart &
Kidd.

COURTNEY, W. L.
The Idea of Tragedy. Brentano.
Old Saws and Modern Instances. Dutton.

CRAIG, GORDON.
On the Art of the Theater. Sergel.
The Theater—Advancing. Little, Brown.
Towards a New Theater. Dutton.

FREYTAG, GUSTAV.
The Technique of the Drama. Griggs.

FYLES, FRANKLIN.
The Theater and Its People. Doubleday, Page.

HALE, EDWARD EVERETT, JR.
Dramatists of To-day. Holt.

HAMILTON, CLAYTON.
The Theory of the Theater. Holt.
Studies in Stagecraft. Holt.
Problems of the Playwright. Holt.
Seen on the Stage. Holt.

HENDERSON, ARCHIBALD.
The Changing Drama. Stewart & Kidd.
European Dramatists. Stewart & Kidd.

HOPKINS, ARTHUR.
How's Your Second Act? Knopf.

IRVING, HENRY.
The Drama. Tait, New York.

IRVING, H. B.
The Drama. Page.

LEWISOHN, LUDWIG.
The Modern Drama. Huebsch.

MATTHEWS, BRANDER.
The Development of the Drama. Scribner.
A Study of the Drama. Houghton Mifflin.
The Principles of Playwriting. Scribner.

MEREDITH, GEORGE.
An Essay on Comedy. Scribner.

MODERWELL, Hiram Kelly.
The Theater of To-day. Lane.

MONKHOUSE, ALLAN.
Books and Plays. Lane.

PALMER, John.
Comedy. Doran.
The Censor and the Theaters. Kennerley.
The Future of the Theater. Bell, London.

PHELPS, WILLIAM LYON.
The Twentieth Century Theater.

PRICE, WILLIAM T.
The Technique of the Drama. Brentano.
The Analysis of Play Construction and Dramatic Principles. W. T. Price.

ROLLAND, ROMAIN.
The People's Theater. Holt.

SHIPMAN, LOUIS EVAN.
The True Adventures of a Play. Kennerley.

STRANG, LEWIS C.
Plays and Players of the Last Quarter Century. Page.

THORNDIKE, ASHLEY H.
    Tragedy. Houghton Mifflin.
VAUGHAN, C. E.
    Types of Tragic Drama. Macmillan.
WOODBRIDGE, ELIZABETH.
    The Drama, Its Law and Technique. Allyn
    and Bacon.

English and Irish Drama:
ARCHER, WILLIAM.
    About the Theater. Unwin.
    English Dramatists of To-day. Sampson Low.
    Study and Stage. Wessels.
    Masks or Faces? Longmans.
    Real Conversations. Heinemann.
BORSA, MARIO.
    The English Stage of To-day. Lane.
BOYD, E. A.
    Ireland's Literary Renaissance. Lane.
    The Contemporary Drama of Ireland. Little,
    Brown.
DICKINSON, T. H.
    The Contemporary Drama of England. Little,
    Brown.
DUKES, ASHLEY.
    Modern Dramatists. Sergel.
FILON, AUGUSTIN.
    The English Stage. Dodd, Mead.
GEORGE, W. L.
    Dramatic Actualities. Sidgwick and Jackson.
GREGORY, LADY AUGUSTA.
    Our Irish Theater. Putnam.

Howe, P. P.
  Dramatic Portraits. Kennerley.
  The Repertory Theater. Kennerley.

Jones, Henry Arthur.
  Renascence of the English Drama. Macmillan.
  The Foundations of a National Drama. Doran.
  The Theater of Ideas. Doran.

Kennedy, J. M.
  Modern English Literature. Stephen Swift,
  London.

Krans, Horatio Sheafe.
  William Butler Yeats and the Irish Literary
  Revival. Doubleday, Page.

McCarthy, Desmond.
  The Court Theater. A. H. Bullen, Stratford-on-
  Avon.

Moore, George.
  Hail and Farewell. Appleton. (3 vols.)
  Impressions and Opinions. Brentano.

Oliver, D. E.
  The English Stage. John Ouseley, London.

Weygandt, Cornelius.
  Irish Plays and Playwrights. Houghton Mifflin.

Yeats, William Butler.
  Ideas of Good and Evil. Macmillan.
  The Cutting of an Agate. Macmillan.

Collected Dramatic Criticism:

Archer, William.
  The Theatrical World. (5 vols.) Walter Scott,
  London.

GREIN, J. T.
Dramatic Criticism. John Long, London, 1899.
Premières of the Year. Macqueen, London, 1900.
Dramatic Criticism. Greening, London, 1901.
Dramatic Criticism. Evelyn Nash, London, 1904.

MONTAGUE, C. E.
Dramatic Values. Macmillan.

SCOTT, CLEMENT.
Drama of Yesterday and To-day. (2 vols.) Macmillan.

SHAW, BERNARD.
Dramatic Opinions and Essays. (2 vols.) Brentano.

E. F. S[PENCE].
Our Stage and Its Critics. Methuen, London.

SYMONS, ARTHUR.
Plays, Acting, and Music. Dutton.

TITTERTON, W. R.
From Theater to Music Hall. Stephen Swift, London.

WALBROOK.
Nights at the Play. Ham-Smith, London.

WALKLEY, A. B.
Frames of Mind. Richards, London.
The Drama and Life. Brentano.
Playhouse Impressions. Unwin, London.
Dramatic Criticism. Murray, London.

Dictionaries, Year-Books, etc.:

ADAMS, WILLIAM D.
A Dictionary of the Drama, A to G, (English and American). Lippincott.

BOSTON Book Co. (Publishers.)
Bulletin of Bibliography.
Modern Drama and Opera, a reading list.

BROWN, FRANK C.
A Selective List of Essays and Books about the Drama and the Theater. Drama League of America.

BROWN, T. ALLSTON.
History of the New York Stage (1732-1901). Dodd, Mead. (3 vols.)

CARSON, LIONEL.
The Stage Year Book. (Appears annually.) London.

CLARENCE, REGINALD.
The Stage Cyclopedia. London.

CLARK, BARRETT H.
Representative One-Act Plays by English and Irish Authors. Little, Brown.

DICKINSON, THOMAS H., Editor.
Chief Contemporary Dramatists. Houghton Mifflin. (Contains twenty modern plays and brief reading lists on Wilde, Pinero, Jones, Galsworthy, Barker, Yeats, Synge, Lady Gergory, Fitch, Moody, Thomas, and Mackaye.)

HINES, DIXIE; and HANAFORD, HARRY PRES-
COTT.
Who's Who in Music and Drama. Hanaford,
New York (1914).

LOVING, PIERRE AND SHAY, FRANK.
Fifty Contemporary One-Act Plays. Stewart &
Kidd. (Satisfies a long-felt want for a handy
collection of the choicest plays produced by
the art theaters all over the world. It is a
complete repertory for a little theater; a volume for the study of the modern drama, a
representative collection of the world's best
short plays.)

MAYORGA, MARGARET.
Representative One-Act Plays by American
Authors. Little, Brown.

MOSES, MONTROSE J.
Representative British Dramas. Little, Brown.

PARKER, JOHN.
Who's Who in the Theater. Isaac Pitman,
London.

PENCE, JAMES HARRY (compiler).
The Magazine and the Drama, an index.
(The Dunlap Society.)

QUINN, A. H.
Representative American Plays. Century Co.

RODEN, ROBERT F.
Later American Plays (1831–1900). (The Dunlap Society.)

American Drama:

ANONYMOUS.
The Truth About the Theater. Stewart & Kidd.

ANDREWS, CHARLTON.
The Drama To-day. Lippincott.

BELASCO, DAVID.
The Theater Through its Stage Door. Harper's.

BURTON, RICHARD.
The New American Drama. Crowell.

CHANDLER, FRANK WADLEIGH.
Aspects of Modern Drama. Macmillan.

CHENEY, SHELDON.
The New Movement in the Theater. Kennerley.

CRAWFORD, MARY CAROLINE.
The Romance of the American Theater. Little, Brown.

DICKINSON, T. H.
The Case of American Drama. Houghton, Mifflin.
The Insurgent Theater. Huebsch.

FROHMAN, DANIEL.
Memories of a Manager. Doubleday, Page.

GOLDMAN, EMMA.
The Social Significance of the Modern Drama. Badger.

HAPGOOD, NORMAN.
The Stage in America (1897–1900). Macmillan.

HORNBLOW, ARTHUR.
A History of the Theater in America. Lippincott.

MACKAYE, PERCY.
The Playhouse and the Play. Macmillan.
The Civic Theater. Kennerley.

MATTHEWS, BRANDER.
A Study of the Drama. Houghton Mifflin.
Inquiries and Opinions. Scribner.
The Historical Novel and Other Essays. Scribner.

MODERWELL, HIRAM KELLEY.
The Theater of To-day. Lane.

MOSES, MONTROSE J.
The American Dramatist. Little, Brown.

Collected Criticism:

EATON, WALTER PRICHARD.
The New Theater, and Others. Small, Maynard.
The American Stage of To-day. Small, Maynard.
Plays and Players. Stewart & Kidd.

HAMILTON, CLAYTON.
Studies in Stagecraft. Holt.
Problems of the Playwright. Holt.
Seen on the Stage. Holt.

MATTHEWS, BRANDER.
Books and Plays. Scribner.

NATHAN, GEORGE JEAN.
  Mr. George Jean Nathan Presents. Knopf.
  The Popular Theater. Knopf.
  Comedians All. Knopf.

NIRDLINGER, CHARLES F.
  Masques and Mummers. De Witt, New York.

RUHL, ARTHUR.
  Second Nights. Scribner.

WINTER, WILLIAM.
  The Wallet of Time. (2 vols.) Moffat, Yard.
  Other Days. Moffat, Yard.
  Shadows of the Stage. (3 vols.) Macmillan.
  The Life and Art of Richard Mansfield.
    (2 vols.) Moffat, Yard.

INDEX